# Decorum

Supervising Editors:

Kristina Gladfelter and Melody Niesen

Associate Editors:
Joseph Alfino
Erinn Metcalf

Contributors:
Rose Gubele
Heather Hughe

D1275390

University of Central

FOUNTAINHEAD
PRESS

Our green initiatives include:

Electronic Products
We deliver products in non-paper form whenever possible. This includes pdf downloadables, flash drives, and CDs.

Electronic Samples
We use Xample, a new electronic sampling system. Instructor samples are sent via a personalized web page that links to PDF downloads.

FSC Certified Printers
All of our printers are certified by the Forest Service Council, which promotes environmentally and socially responsible management of the world's forests. This program allows consumer groups, individual consumers, and businesses to work together hand-in-hand to promote responsible use of the world's forests as a renewable and sustainable resource.

Recycled Paper
Most of our products are printed on a minimum of 30% post-consumer waste recycled paper.

Support of Green Causes
When we do print, we donate a portion of our revenue to green causes. Listed below are a few of the organizations that have received donations from Fountainhead Press. We welcome your feedback and suggestions for contributions, as we are always searching for worthy initiatives.
Rainforest 2 Reef
Environmental Working Group

Cover photo by William C. Gleason

Design by Susan Moore

Books may be purchased for educational purposes.

For information, please call or write:

1-800-586-0330

Fountainhead Press
Southlake, TX 76092

Web Site: www.fountainheadpress.com
E-mail: customerservice@fountainheadpress.com

Revised Second Edition

ISBN: 978-1-68036-270-1

Printed in the United States of America.

# Table of Contents

# Part I:
# Contexts for Writing

# Writing at the University of Central Missouri

## What is Composition?

When students think of writing in college, they often think about following a prompt, typing up their essay (usually late at night and on too little sleep), and handing it in to their professor. After viewing the grade and comments, the process often ends there. However, that view of writing is limited. Writing can take on a variety of forms and serve a variety of purposes. The world is constantly shifting: technology's influence expands, norms change, and new information surfaces. The definition of composition likewise shifts, and it becomes far more than words lying dormant on a page.

So, then, what is decorum?

As the title of your book suggests, decorum and writing are closely connected. The modern definition of decorum is rules we must follow to achieve propriety when communicating or interacting with others within specific contexts. One of the first definitions of decorum, developed by prominent Roman rhetorician Cicero, is less rule-based than the contemporary idea. Decorum, in Cicero's view, is more liberating than confining, because it helps us determine how to negotiate with others. It is, therefore, a term that we need to understand. In our lives today, means of communication are everywhere (cell phones, social media, blogs, etc.), but the act of connecting with others is becoming increasingly complicated. In academia, communication is even more of a challenge. As you move from high school into college, you will have to negotiate the change in decorum as you encounter different expectations. Understanding how to determine decorum will help you navigate your changing situation as you move from college into graduate school and/or work environments as well.

So, this textbook is not a book about determining the "rules of decorum." It is a book that will help guide you (the student) in the process of communicating and making connections between people and ideas. The main focus of this book is writing, but the principles within can be applied to reading, critical thinking, speech, and other skills as well. These skills aren't limited to your composition class. You compose every day: Tweets, Facebook posts, blogs, captions for photos, private journals, and more. Each mode of writing carries with it different rules and expectations. For example, a tweet can't exceed 140 characters. In a private journal entry, you know that you're only writing for yourself, which means you might not worry about standard writing conventions. Similarly, a formal essay probably shouldn't contain inappropriate, personal content. Composition involves knowing how to conduct oneself in each writing situation. This situational awareness is, essentially, *Decorum*.

## How is College Writing Different from Other Writing?

While your high school teachers definitely helped prepare you for college writing, there are many different elements that you must take into consideration when writing for college courses; your composition teacher will help you navigate these conventions and identify the appropriate decorum for a variety of situations. Some of these conventions are listed below.

### The Rhetorical Triangle
*(See Chapter 10.)*

#### Author

Some people resist thinking of themselves as authors, but anyone who writes is an author; anyone who wants to send a message through any means of communication is an author. The author's purpose depends upon the goal and context of the written piece.

#### Message

The message is what the author wants the audience to understand. A message can range from simple to complex. Nuances and connotations of words can add levels of meaning to a text, which might help the audience to receive the message in different ways.

#### Audience

Students often assume that teachers are the only ones who will read their work, but what if that isn't always the case? The audience is the person, or people, to whom the author wants to speak. The audience can be any size—

from one person to thousands of people. Imagining a broader audience for an essay can help you better address the decorum of that situation.

### Context

The context is the situation within which the author's message occurs. The kind of language an author uses, the tone, and the style all differ depending on the context. The messages that authors send to academic audiences, for example, are far different than the ones sent to the general public. Also, different academic disciplines have different terms and styles that they commonly use.

## Style
*(See Chapter 8.)*

Today, the word "style" is used in a number of contexts: fashion, written formats, and lifestyles. Written prose style reflects the education, experience, and habits of thought of the writer. Style is also part of the argumentative and emotional design of an essay. Well-chosen words and well-crafted sentences have the potential to evoke emotion, persuade a reluctant audience, and communicate a message more clearly and effectively.

## Critical Thinking
*(See Chapter 2.)*

Effective composition depends on clear and original thinking. While you may be tempted to simply skim the surface and take the easiest, most obvious route when writing, it's important to remember that every writing experience brings an opportunity to offer new and original insights. Composition provides a platform for you to say something, learn something, and contribute to a conversation in order to make your voice heard.

## MO Grammar

MO Grammar is a custom program developed by the English & Philosophy Department at the University of Central Missouri. The program is intended to help you review and polish your grammar skills, knowledge, and practice. Because the program was designed by your instructors with you in mind, it is even more important for you to utilize the resource as it will help you be more successful. Good grammar is essential to communicating your intended message to a specific audience.

## Common Reader

One Campus, One Book is a common reading program at UCM that is meant to engage all of our students and campus community in a shared, academically-driven experience during the fall semester. This initiative is intended to bring meaningful conversations on relevant, complex subjects beyond the classroom and into your daily life. The common reading program will culminate in a visit by the book's author to our campus in the fall semester.

By bringing an author to campus whose book will be included in first-year composition courses, this program will engage you with a text that addresses a contemporary social issue, encourage you to extend critical and rhetorical analysis to your life beyond the classroom, and help you synthesize what may seem like competing academic subjects, creating an interdisciplinary spirit of curiosity on campus. *Pleiades*, a journal of new writing published by UCM, is also a great resource to learn more about various subjects as well as find book reviews.

## Course Goals and Outcomes
### *(see Appendix.)*

This course meets General Education Competency One: Writing with clarity and purpose using appropriate conventions of format, structure, and documentation.

You will learn that writing is a cyclical process that includes drafting, revision, and editing. You will be exposed to formal and informal writing, write multiple drafts of essays, and have at least two individual tutorials with your instructor.

For further details and specific information, consult your course syllabus.

## Academic Literacy

Your general education writing courses add to your **academic literacy**, and academic literacy is essential in order to achieve academic success. Academic literacy includes traditional educational elements such as reading, writing, listening, speaking, and critical thinking. In the age of Photoshop, instant news, and clickbait, it's more important than ever to view texts with a critical eye and evaluate what we consume before believing it. Academic literacy also includes habits of mind that can advance academic success;

these habits include curiosity and skepticism about new ideas, courage to embrace changing ideas, and participation in intellectual discussions. Being able to convey your ideas clearly and to listen and respond to the diverse views of others is also part of being academically literate. You will practice all of these skills in Composition I.

However, the core requirements in the educational system of the United States have recently changed, and these changes have added to what constitutes academic literacy. To be academically literate, *you must be responsible for your own learning and engage in self-advocacy* when what you have learned, or have not learned, does not meet the educational and workplace goals you have set for yourself. Finally, academic literacy includes most basic and some advanced technological skills such as word processing, e-mail use, and the fundamentals of Web-based research. Successful students know that their engagement with complex ideas underpins their membership in the academic community, and they also practice the 21st-century literacies that make up academic literacy as a whole.

Learning to read and write effectively for all occasions, and especially for the specialized writing of your discipline and future career, is one of the keys to getting and keeping a job. In a recent survey by the Partnership for 21st Century Skills, when employers were asked what makes recent college graduates ready to hire, more than 90 percent of the employers said that writing and critical thinking are "very important" for success. In the same survey, however, these same employers described only 16 percent of their new hires as having excellent written communication skills and 28 percent as having excellent critical thinking skills (*P21*). The 2004 College Board's National Commission on Writing confirmed that writing is an entry-level skill that new employees are expected to have but that a third of workers fail to meet the writing requirements of their jobs.

Because academic literacy skills are now considered so essential, you should be prepared to have them tested at job interviews with problem-set writing questions, case-based interviews, mini-project assignments, and role-playing exercises, all of which require mastery of writing and critical thinking skills. Thus, the writing in Composition I prepares you for your future, not only your general education courses and your discipline-specific courses.

## Strategies 1.1

### Transferring Your Literacy to Different Situations

1. **Become smart about texts (have textual intelligence)**

   a. Learn how texts are structured, how different grammatical structures affect readers, what text format is needed, and how text can appear in print, visual, or audio formats.

   b. Be knowledgeable about point of view, the verb tense that is expected in different disciplines, and how organization can influence your reader.

2. **Look for contextual clues in your writing assignments**

   a. **Contextualize**: When you encounter a new writing assignment, reflect on past assignments and how some of the tools or knowledge you used then can be applied to the current assignment.

   b. **Decontextualize**: After you complete a writing assignment, reflect on the tools you used and knowledge about writing you gained. Be prepared to access this information for future writing assignments.

3. **Think about thinking (have meta-cognitive awareness)**

   a. After you complete a piece of writing, think about what you thought as you did your prewriting, writing, and postwriting.

   b. Keep a writer's log or commonplace book and jot down your reflections about how you discovered your thesis or found your research materials.

4. **Investigate all sides**

   a. Look at topics and arguments from multiple sides.

   b. Practice developing differing or conflicting interpretations and arguments, and then support these divergent ideas with well-structured support.

5. **Learn to identify genres (type of writing and format of writing)**

   a. Consider the type of writing that you are doing. Is it persuasive or argumentative? Informative or narrative?

   b. Also consider the form or shape your writing takes. Is there a particular format involved, such as memo form or research paper form, that is used in the discipline or in the work environment?

6. **Consider target audiences**

   a. As you write, identify the target audience. Investigate and keep track of the people who make up the discourse community (ingroup) of your audience. Look at other writings that have been written for that audience. Are there particular terms or phrases that are used for them? Is writing aimed at them written in active (The pilot flew the plane.) or passive voice (The plane was flown by the pilot.)?

   b. When you write something new, look back at other pieces of writing and reflect on what you learned about the audience. Apply what you learned to the new writing, or if the audience is different, use similar strategies to reflect on the new audience.

   c. Keep track of what type of research or documentation is needed in each piece of writing you do. Return to earlier pieces to refresh your memory about the particular research or documentation necessary.

7. **Create writing goals that fit you and your future courses or workplaces**

   a. Figure out the big questions you want to explore through your education, and focus on these questions as you choose writing topics.

   b. Connect each assignment to where you are going next. Reflect on what you can carry with you from the current writing to the next step in your education.

8. **Revise, redo, repeat**

   a. Learn from everything you write. Reflect on the comments given to you about your writing, and use your new knowledge to revise, even if you will not turn in the revision for a grade.

   b. Collect your papers at the end of the semester. Keep them in a folder or binder, and return to them when you have a new writing assignment that is similar.

9. **Be an independent learner**

   a. Whenever you complete a writing assignment or activity, reflect on what you learned and how that may relate to your future educational or work goals.

   b. Write to learn. Whenever you read or think about something new, write about it as well.

c. Learn to write. Writing courses will never cover everything you need to know. Read your textbooks, and then independently study what was not covered.

d. Take notes, ask questions, and read a range of texts outside of your courses.

10. **Know your discipline**

a. How do members in your discipline find information? Where is the information available online? What research strategies are common?

b. Is collaboration common in your area of study? If so, how is that collaboration done, and how is writing credit usually shared?

## Assignment 1.1

### Define Modern Composition

1. Establish a persona as an author (an elementary school student, your high school English teacher, etc).

2. Select a specific audience (your grandmother, Mo the UCM mule, an alien from outer space).

3. Write your definition of modern composition.

4. Establish a specific context (explaining your college courses, the kind of writing you do online, etc).

5. Share your definition with your peers.

# Chapter 2

# Tips for Reading and Writing in College

## Academic Reading

Reading is essential to academic literacy. Reading provides you with an understanding of vocabulary, grammar, sentence structure, and text structure (genre). The more you read and the more varied you are in your reading, the more authentic language input you give your brain to absorb and process, allowing you to foster the development of a broader vocabulary, richer sentence variety, and rhetorical maturity. Reading also provides you with opportunities for cultural inquiry and awareness, including an introduction to the specialized writing you will be reading in your chosen field. Most of all, though, reading allows you to obtain content information about subjects that you are studying in depth.

When you read to learn, you are reading to comprehend and retain information more effectively. One of the tenets of reading to learn is to create a vocabulary that will make your thoughts more tangible so you can organize and analyze them effectively. Whether it is a general education course or a course in your major, your instructor will usually assign reading to help you understand lecture material or prepare you for writing assignments or exams that will employ your ideas.

To be a successful writer, you need to be able to read varied and extensive material with a high command of understanding. Some reading assignments may be low risk, such as looking over material prior to a lecture, and some may be of a higher risk, such as reading research essays that you will critically evaluate in terms of their usefulness for your own research paper. Whatever the risk, the main purpose behind any assigned course reading is to make you more comfortable with thinking critically about key concepts.

## Learning to Read Critically

To be an effective reader, you should be an **active reader**. You need to bring all your knowledge to the forefront and use it as you process new material for understanding. Good readers engage with the text as if in a conversation by asking questions and searching for answers as they read. They observe how they are interacting with the text by taking notes or keeping track of main concepts and important information. One of the most important ways for you to become an effective reader—one who is able to observe details, recall facts, and come to conclusions—is to apply strategies that will help you process what you read.

Different disciplines may have diverse classes, distinct types of information, and disciplinary-specific types of writing, but they all include reading. When you are assigned reading in a course, you are a scholar, and scholarly reading is quite different from reading for pleasure. You must be critical to be an effective scholarly reader. One component of being critical begins with asking questions about why the reading was assigned.

The following questions will help you understand the assignment's purpose:

- How does this reading fit in with the objectives of the course?
- How does this reading address the themes of the course?
- How does this reading relate to what is currently being covered in the course?
- Is the reading a critical part of an assignment that will follow?

Once you understand why a reading has been assigned, consider how your instructor wants you to read, process, and analyze the reading. If you are not certain, it is a good idea to ask your instructor how you should manage the assigned reading and process it for understanding. The amount of time you allocate to the reading will depend on how much you want to absorb from the reading.

Use these questions to determine how you want to read; the further down the list, the more time it will take you to process the reading for full understanding:

- Was this reading assigned for entertainment?
- Was this reading assigned to grasp a certain message?
- Was this reading assigned to find an important detail?
- Was this reading assigned to answer a specific question?

- Was this reading assigned to be evaluated?
- Was this reading assigned to apply its concepts to something else?

Using active reading strategies improves comprehension, retention, and recall. Some of these strategies may already be familiar to you. Whether the following are new to you or not, it is a good idea to have an arsenal of strategies that work. The reading process can be separated into three primary areas: prereading, reading actively, and postreading. Depending on what kind of reader you are, you should be able to choose at least a few strategies in each area to help you become a more critical reader, a key component of academic literacy.

## Strategies 2.1

### Prereading

1. **Consider what you have already brainstormed regarding the reasons your instructor assigned this reading.**

2. **Know your discipline's common organization for articles and books.** Each field has its own practice, and knowing yours will help you know where to find abstracts or conclusions that will help you review the material.

3. **Read the preface and introduction.** Oftentimes, the author or editor will present or review important points for you.

4. **Preview and predict what the reading will be about.**
   a. Look at the table of contents, and review the headings and subheadings for the assigned reading.
   b. Write a short journal entry that describes what you know about the topics that are listed in the headings.
   c. Draft some questions you have about the topic.
   d. Use a K-W-L chart by creating columns headed with "What I Know," "What I Want to Know," and "What I Learned." Fill in the first two columns prior to reading and the last after you finish.

5. **Skim and scan the reading before you start fully reading.** Look at how many pages the reading is, how many sections there are, how long the sections are, and what types of headings and subheadings there are.

6. **Create reading goals and develop a plan to split up what has been assigned.** You can do this in a journal, on notebook paper, on your calendar, or in the table of contents.

7. **Choose specific times to read that are convenient for you, and plan enough time to finish a full section.** Figure out how many pages you can read in an hour, count up your assigned reading, and then make a realistic plan of attack.

### Strategies 2.2
#### Reading Actively

1. **Break it up.** Read for 30 to 45 minutes, and then review what you have read before taking a short break. An effective strategy is to read for 30–45 minutes, review for 5 minutes, and then take a break for 5 minutes.

2. **Read section by section.** It is best to stop when there is a natural break in the reading material. This will help later when you organize your notes, since they will already be focused on one section at a time.

3. **Circle new terms and underline their definitions.** Use a circle or some other graphic tool to help you note new terms as you read and note them later as you return to review the reading. If the term is not defined in the text, look it up and note the definition near the term in the reading, if possible. Consider creating a "vocabulary terms" page at the beginning of your notebook or binder, and note both the term and its definition when you first encounter them.

4. **Annotate your text.** Draw attention to main ideas or important points by underlining, highlighting, circling, or using asterisks or other graphic reminders. Use a pen or pencil, rather than a highlighter; you'll have less chance of marking excessively. Use the margin for your own notes; questioning, identifying, and/or summarizing content; and ultimately, having a conversation with the text. If you are marking too much, it means you aren't able to select main points and important details. Highlighting more than 20 percent of the text means this strategy isn't working for you.

5. **Read difficult sections out loud, or take turns reading out loud with a classmate.** This will help you process the important information in more than one way since it adds the audio element to the visual.

6. **Create a bulleted list of main ideas as you read, or use an informal or formal outline method.** You might also use a cluster approach to keep notes about related ideas together.

7. **Create a timeline to keep track of dates, especially when reading literature or when reading about history.**

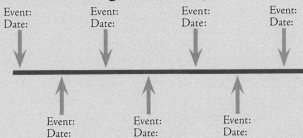

8. **Draw helpful pictures or diagrams in your notes, especially when you want to depict relationships between one character or idea to another.**

9. **Visualize different sections or ideas by using different colored pens, pencils, or highlighters.**

10. **Take notes as you read.** Write down questions next to the material as you read, or keep a detailed commonplace book with questions, and be sure to include the page number of the material to which they refer.

**Strategies 2.3**

**Postreading**

1. **Answer reading questions that your instructor has given you, or check the end of the chapter or the book's website for helpful questions.**

2. **Mark information in your notes that connects to your instructor's lectures or other class materials.** Bring your reading notes to class, and highlight any information from the book that your instructor covers again in class or asks questions about.

3. **Turn your linear notes into a chart, table, outline, or any other graphic that will help you process the information more quickly.** Your teacher will likely provide a variety of graphic organizer styles; however, you can always search for the right one for you online.

4. **Read particularly challenging sections again, or reread as needed to answer study questions.**

5. **Use special strategies for difficult material.**

a. Reread. Sometimes rereading is all it takes to grasp something you didn't understand the first time around.

b. Stop reading after each paragraph or section, and write your response, or paraphrase or summarize what you have read using your own words.

c. Discuss the reading with a classmate, create a study group, or go visit your instructor during office hours.

d. Create a flow chart of how ideas in each section or paragraph relate to each other.

e. Take a break from your reading and return when you are refreshed. Sometimes, a cup of coffee or a good night's sleep will help you understand what was eluding you.

## Academic Writing

Writing is power. It is the power to write successful essays and test answers in school and the power to write effective memos and reports in business. It is the power to present your own point of view or to disagree with someone else's. It is the power to communicate. We are all writers; we write e-mails, blog posts, job applications, proposals, reviews, and requests. We answer important requests in writing; we respond to complaints in writing. And, overall, life is just easier for those who can write well.

Writing helps us do the following:

- Communicate our thoughts and feelings
- Think more deeply and critically
- Discover and shape new ideas
- Consider ethical issues
- Improve our performance
- Prepare us for what comes after school
- Map out a meaningful life

## Learning to be Successful at Academic Writing

Your other instructors will assume that you are already a proficient writer, able to think critically about the topics you read about or discuss in class and to skillfully present your knowledge and viewpoints. Even though your instructors may refer to the writing process or successful writing traits, they will often consider this review material. To insure that you are prepared for those expectations, be proactive and take responsibility for your Composition experience by following the steps below.

1. **Read the syllabus and each assignment thoroughly. Highlight due dates and other important clues.** Invest in a printed calendar just for your writing class, or create one on your computer and print it out. Build a writing process schedule that allows at least two to three weeks of incremental work leading up to the final draft of each assigned essay.

2. **Know your instructor and yourself. Early in the semester, ask your instructor about his or her writing "do's and don'ts."** Write these down, and look at them before you turn in a writing assignment. Writing classes require a lot of reading, excellent attendance and participation, and a knack for sticking to schedules. Anticipate which of these requirements are likely to cause you problems, and rework your schedule accordingly.

3. **Trust yourself.** Academic papers may be formal, but they should still reflect your own voice and views. Do not pretend to be someone you are not when you write.

4. **Be sure to use all the resources available to you. In the first week of class, find out where your instructor's office is and what his or her office hours are.** Find UCM's writing center. Locate a 24-hour computer lab. Take a tour of the library. Locate a printer that is close to your classroom.

5. **Do not procrastinate.** Do your reading when assigned—earlier if possible. Since writing is viewed as a process, some instructors grade both process material and your final essay draft. Be sure to complete each step of the writing process on time; this will help you arrive at a polished final essay draft before or by the due date.

6. **Attend all classes and participate in class discussions.** This seems obvious, but after years of being in high school, you might embrace the freedom of collegiate scheduling too much and run your absences to the limit allowed. Not being in class is the easiest way to ruin your class grade, even if attendance and participation are a small percentage of the total grade. Being in class allows you to learn the instructor's pet peeves, tackle small parts of writing assignments with your peers, and learn more about topics through class discussion. It also allows your instructor to get to know you better and fine tune their support. For more details refer to the course syllabus.

7. **Keep track of instructor and peer comments.** Use a grid or a small notebook to collect instructor or peer comments about your writing, whether the comments are about content, logic, organization, vocabulary, or grammar. After a few assignments, you will be able to analyze your own writing, and you will know what you need to work on to improve the next essay.

8. **Be flexible.** Each writing instructor and group of students has a combined different experience than any other. Understand that the advice given to you by your eighth grade teacher or advanced placement tutor is not the only good advice you may receive. Build up your writing knowledge base with each piece of writing advice you are given. Sometimes this means that you will have to consider opposing viewpoints—there is more than one way to become a good writer. There is always more to learn; academic growth is always possible.

9. **Build up your reading muscle.** Complete assigned readings carefully before participating in class discussions or writing textual analysis essays. If you do not read much outside of your classwork, now is the time to begin reading the newspaper once a day, making your way through a bestselling nonfiction or fiction book over the break, and/or dedicating yourself to reading a reporter's blog each day or week. Do not restrict your reading—the more you read, the more tools you will have to write.

10. **Write, write, write, and write some more.** Any type of writing will help you become a better writer, so do not limit yourself to essay assignments. Work through all the process assignments for Composition I, and use these same tools for other classes as well. Respond to prompts or questions given on Blackboard or outside blogs or news stories. Write a letter home once a month. Each time you work on your global writing skills (content, organization, and vocabulary) and your local writing skills (grammar, mechanics, and formatting), you help yourself become a better writer.

## Learning to Identify Academic Writing Assignments

Writing assignments can vary from a five-minute prewriting activity to a longer research essay or even a multimedia document.

### Process Work
### *(See Chapters 3 and 9.)*

Most writing classes will include process work that will be graded or counted in some way; instructors in other academic classes may not grade process work but still expect you to do such work as a precursor to meeting about or submitting a writing project. Process work may include any activity that helps you brainstorm, organize, review, revise, edit, or proofread your essay. These activities may take place during class time, making good attendance necessary and worthwhile.

### In-class or Timed Writing Assignments

Writing assignments may include in-class or timed essays, such as a get-to-know-you writing activity or reflection on the day's reading. In-class writing does not usually allow time for substantial revision and editing. If given an in-class essay, break the time allowed into short blocks that mimic the parts of the process for an out-of-class essay. If you have 60 minutes, use 5–10 minutes to brainstorm and outline, 30–40 minutes to write the first draft, 5–10 minutes to revise for global concerns, and 5–10 minutes to edit for local concerns. If you are writing on a computer, print out a copy of the paper, if possible, to revise and edit offline. Then, add changes, correct spelling and typos, and print your final draft. Even in a tight writing situation, it pays to make time for both revising and editing.

### Out-of-Class Essay Assignments

The typical essay associated with a writing class is the out-of-class essay assignment given to you about two or three weeks before the essay is due, or possibly months in advance for extended research projects. It is important to analyze the assignment sheet in depth as soon as you receive it and work out a writing plan. Often, this assignment sheet will also detail step-by-step activities, such as due dates for drafts or revising/editing workshops. Mark these dates on your calendar, and complete each step of the process to ensure a well-developed essay.

### Multimedia Assignments

A writing class may also include activities that you might not automatically associate with writing. However, writing is an important component of some multimodal and process assignments, such as presenting or responding to ideas in emails, class discussion boards, and social networking sites. Multimedia assignments in a writing class can also include designing Web documents and oral presentations.

## Kinds of Academic Writing Assignments

Not all writing is persuasive, but all writing involves the interplay between author, audience, and message, so it all occurs within a context. *In A Theory of Discourse*, James Kinneavy argues that there are four basic kinds of writing: persuasive, expressive, informative, and literary. Each form of writing emphasizes a different dynamic between the audience, author, and message. Expressive writing focuses on the author, who wants to write about what he or she feels is important. On the other hand, informative writing focuses on the subject matter, and the purpose of the genre is to inform. Persuasive writing focuses greatly on the audience, because the goal is to change the audience's viewpoint. Literary writing is a specialized genre that focuses on the features of the writing; it is taught primarily in creative writing courses and studied in literature classes.

In college, students will encounter expressive, informative, and persuasive writing most frequently. Below is a list of some common assignments and how they can be classified.

**Table 2.1: Expressive, Informative, and Persuasive Writing**

| Genre | Description | Kinds of Assignments |
|-------|-------------|----------------------|
| **Expressive** | Focuses on the author, and the purpose is self-expression | Journal assignments<br>Reaction papers<br>Personal stories |
| **Informative** | Focuses on the message, and the purpose is to explain | Research papers (some, not all)<br>Synthesis papers<br>Book reports<br>Lab reports |
| **Persuasive** | Focuses on the audience, and the goal is to persuade | Argumentative papers<br>Argumentative research papers<br>Position papers |

Many assignments fall between the three types of writing listed above. For example, research papers almost always lean toward informative writing, but some are argumentative (as noted). Even argumentative research papers focus on informing the audience, though. Also, true expressive writing is rare in college; to be completely expressive, a piece of writing needs to be completely focused on the author alone. However, every college writing assignment has an audience, so the author must consider that audience even when writing expressively.

In fact, each college writing assignment, whatever the style or purpose, emphasizes audience to some degree. Students often imagine their teacher as their audience. This is partly true, but many teachers want students to imagine a broader academic audience for their work. Your teacher may tell you a specific audience to imagine as well.

| Strategies 2.4 |
| --- |
| **Deconstructing the Assignment Sheet** |

- Read the assignment sheet more than once, highlighting different types of information with different colors. Be sure to highlight due dates, genre/media requirements, and formatting requirements.

- Return to the assignment sheet at various times throughout the writing process, double-checking that you are on task.

- If the assignment gives information about required writing process steps (such as brainstorming activities, multiple drafts, revising or editing workshops) note these on your calendar immediately.

- Pay close attention to important words (such as "requirement," "tip," "note," "NB," or "hint") or formatting (bolded words, italics) that are used to focus your attention on particular tasks.

- Be sure to ask for explanations if you do not understand something about the assignment. Visit your instructor for a tutorial or during their office hours.

## Beyond the Classroom

## Sharing, Presenting, and Publishing

Motivation is key to becoming a good writer, but motivation can prove elusive when someone else is requiring you to write. One way to help yourself become a better writer is to go beyond writing for a class grade. Find a way to share your writing in other venues. Sometimes an instructor will build this type of incentive into a writing class syllabus by asking you to read your final draft to others in the class or by posting the final draft online for others—your classmates or outsiders—to read. If this is not available to you, consider some other ways to share your writing outside of class:

- Ask your instructor to allow you and your peers to each share one essay aloud in class on the final day.

- Ask your instructor if you can collect essays from those who volunteer and publish them in bound-copy form at your university's printing office or a local copy shop.

- Submit your essay to the English Department student-published magazine, *Arcade*.

- Submit your argumentative essay to the opinion section of a local newspaper such as *The Muleskinner, The Warrensburg Daily Star-Journal,* or *The Kansas City Star.*

- Submit your essay to a favorite blog or on-line magazine.

- Write your essay with scholarship applications in mind. Since scholarships ask applicants to describe their educational history or an important learning experience, these writing tasks may overlap with narrative or descriptive essays you write in class.

- Ask your former high school English teacher if you and some of your peers can visit his or her class to share your writing as samples of the writing students should expect in college.

## Literacy in the Workplace

The common core of literacies that make up academic literacy are also essential in the workplace. How effectively you are able to transfer the skills and knowledge that you acquire in college is key to your success in the workplace. As Deborah Brandt, a widely recognized literacy scholar, shares in her 2001 book, *Literacy in American Lives*, "Literacy is a valued commodity in the U.S. economy, a key resource in gaining profit and edge" (21). So, to get a job and keep that job, literacy skills, general knowledge, and specific disciplinary knowledge are all necessary. The 2007 report, "Tough Choices or Tough Times," published by the National Center of Education and the Economy (NCEE), confirms that "this is a world in which a very high level of preparation in reading, writing, speaking, mathematics, science, literature, history, and the arts will be indispensable . . . in which comfort with ideas and abstractions is the passport to a good job, in which creativity and innovation are the keys to a good life."

Transfer of skills and knowledge, then, is not only important as you transition from your general education courses to courses in your major; it is also vitally significant as you transition into the workforce.

Being able to decontexualize what you learn in your classes and then recontextualize those skills and that knowledge into the new environment of your workplace will determine your future success. Thus, you need to be constantly aware of what you are learning and how it can support your life and work goals.

## Assignment 2.1

### Keep a Commonplace Book

Ancient rhetoricians performed speeches with little warning, often to advertise their services as teachers of rhetoric. Thus, they frequently memorized arguments about specific topics that could be adapted to the audience and situation on a moment's notice. They called these memorized arguments "commonplaces." **Commonplace books** are an outgrowth of the Greek concept of commonplaces, but they are a little different. They became popular in the Middle Ages as notebooks in which individuals would write down quotes or ideas about a particular topic.

For thousands of years, people have been keeping commonplace books, a kind of journal or diary in which the author includes quotes, drawings, and images. These notations might later be used to generate an idea for a composition.

In more modern times, people have created commonplace books in the form of scrapbooks in which they collect quotes as well as drawings and clippings. Thus, they become a record of a person's intellectual life and can be saved for later reference.

For this class, take a notebook, perhaps one with a colorful or interesting cover, and keep notes, quotes, vocabulary words, and clippings related to the topics discussed in class. As your instructor directs, this commonplace book may be graded as evidence of class participation or it may be a private journal. Take a look at the commonplace books shown here for ideas.

Be creative and enjoy adapting this ancient journal form to record ideas that interest you.

# Part II:
# Elements of Writing

# Planning and Drafting

Peter Elbow is a well-known researcher who writes about college-level writing. In *Writing with Power*, he calls trying to write an essay correctly perfectly the first time a dangerous method "because it puts more pressure on you and depends for its success on everything running smoothly" (42). Let's face it, though. Most writing tasks do not run smoothly, and turning in an essay that you just wrote overnight is definitely a dangerous method, especially when it comes to grades. In the late 1960s, many composition instructors began to treat writing an essay as a process (just like reading), rather than just as a product to be assigned, collected, and graded. **Process writing** classes teach you about and give you the time needed to plan, draft, revise, edit, and proofread your essay before turning it in for a grade.

The process of writing, though, is not a simple linear activity; it is often cyclical and redundant, with writers returning to various stages in the writing process before arriving at the final draft. Each writer has a unique writing process, so even though you  will be introduced to all the different stages of the writing

Figure 3.1: **Cyclical Process of Writing**

process, you may use them differently than another writer in your class. This is one of the ways every writer is unique.

# Brainstorming and Planning

> "Good fortune is what happens when opportunity meets with planning."
>
> —Thomas Edison

The writing process begins before writing the actual paper itself. Brainstorming is the first of many steps that comprise the writing process. If you examine the time it takes to effectively brainstorm and produce a topic for an essay, you will soon realize it is never a good idea to wait until the night before to begin writing a paper. Another strategy to remember is that we write best when we write about topics we are interested in and familiar with. Don't forget that writing is like painting in that it is a very individualized process. Someone can show us how to apply paint to a canvas, but, eventually, we must make these acts our own by adding our own touches.

You can come up with ideas for essays in many ways; however, if you are stuck and cannot find a topic to use, brainstorming, as part of the prewriting or planning you do, can help narrow down general ideas into a focused topic and then help you decide what to use as supporting details. You may already have your own style of prewriting; however, experiment with different methods to find what best suits your style or the assignment at hand.

## Freewriting

You should think of **freewriting** as a "no holds barred" type of brain-storming. When you freewrite, begin by allotting yourself a specific amount of time, such as 10 to 15 minutes. This technique is more constructive when you already have a general subject or an idea for your topic. However, freewriting also can be used to generate ideas for topics. Begin by simply writing. Write whatever comes into your mind. Do not be concerned with punctuation, grammar, or complete sentences. Use symbols or question marks in place of words that you cannot come up with automatically. If you cannot think of anything to write, simply jot down the phrase "I don't know" until you begin writing other words. Remember, this does not have to make sense to anyone else because only you will read it. This writing should be as stress-free as possible.

Here is an example done in three minutes with the topic of peace:

> I only have three minutes to come up with something decent to
> write about. This is stupid. This is not peaceful this is stressful.
> <u>Peace</u> is not writing under pressure. Peace is <u>being barefoot on grass</u>
> <u>by a lake or hearing people laugh</u>. Besides, who can think of peace
> with all of the atrocities in the world? Peace is <u>not war</u>. Peace is the
> <u>absence of war</u>, but maybe it is more than what it isn't. Peace is rep-
> resented by <u>doves, white flags, smiles, and happiness</u>. Peace is also
> represented by <u>a peace sign</u> or <u>holding up two fingers</u>. But I guess
> peace doesn't have to be related to war. It can be associated with
> <u>one's mindset, one's life</u>, or anything that we come into contact
> with in our daily lives.

Once your time is up, sit back, and look at what you have written. Go back
and read your paragraph again, underlining potential topics and subtopics.
Separate out the promising phrases, organize these ideas, and then expand
them.

## Looping

**Looping** is a variation of freewriting. It can be a more constructive brainstorming exercise for those who need a little more focus than freewriting
provides. This technique works best when you already have a general topic
in mind.

For example, you have been assigned to write on your definition of war.
Take out several sheets of paper and begin to freewrite as defined earlier.
When time is up, read over what you have written, and try to pinpoint a
central idea. Perhaps it is the idea that you liked best for whatever reason.
It may simply be an idea that stands out to you. Put this thought or idea
in one sentence below the freewriting. This is called your center of gravity
statement. This completes loop number one.

To begin loop number two, begin freewriting from the previous paragraph's
center of gravity statement. Freewrite for another 10 minutes. Upon
completion of this freewriting session, you will once again assess what
you have written and extract a compelling or important idea that emerged
from your writing. Write this main idea below your freewriting. This is your
second center of gravity statement. Now, begin freewriting from the second
center of gravity statement.

Example of Loop Number 1:

> War is chaos, fighting, and mental anguish. Our traditional definition of war encompasses historical "wars" such as the Revolutionary War, the Civil War, World War I, World War II, and Vietnam just to name a few. War has been a massive part of societies for centuries. War is death, destruction, and bombing. However, I don't think war has to be defined in terms of actual countries physically fighting one another. <u>Wars are waged every day in people's hearts, minds, and lives.</u>

Example of Loop Number 2:

> Wars are waged every day in people's hearts, minds, and lives. The definition of war exceeds beyond the boundaries of our usual definition. War is loneliness, heartbreak, mental illness, daily adversity, and struggles. We normally think of war as having heroes and fantastic stories of bravery. <u>However, if war is defined as doing battle against a foe that is challenging one's established way of life, then loneliness, heartbreak, mental illness, disease, adversity, and struggles can fit easily within the definition of war.</u>

You should continue this looping process until you are satisfied and comfortable with the topic you have generated.

## Journaling

Sometimes, instructors will lead you toward a topic by assigning journals. The Commonplace Book (Assignment 2.1) is one example of a journaling assignment: informal writings that allow you to take a vague idea and write about it. Some journal assignments, like the Commonplace Book, ask you to respond to reading assignments, allowing you to follow an idea or a hunch without worrying about penalty. Think of these journals as a more controlled version of freewriting. Once you complete a journal entry, you can set it aside for a time and come back to it at a later date when you are rested and ready to approach the topic once again.

Here is an example of a journal assignment asking students to write their initial impression of William Faulkner's "A Rose for Emily."

> When I read Faulkner's "A Rose for Emily," I was initially appalled. Miss Emily is clearly sick as she murdered Homer Baron and kept his body in the upper room locked away from the rest of the world. However, I was looking through a scrapbook today and was shocked

at what I found. There, in that scrapbook were pressed flowers, pictures, ticket stubs, and other mementos. Only then did it occur to me that I was acting as Miss Emily had acted. I saved mementos and pictures of a special time that would otherwise be lost forever with nothing to show for it but a memory. I was, just as Miss Emily did, capturing a moment. I suppose it should be noted that Miss Emily had suffered some tragic events in her life and did not have the proper outlets by which to express her heartbreak and loneliness. She merely acts in the only manner she finds effective. In this respect, Faulkner's story demonstrates Miss Emily as a profoundly sympathetic character.

As you can see in this example, the writer's opinion of Miss Emily changed as she reflected on the story. Changes in perspective or thought within in a single journal entry signal that you are thinking critically about a text. After writing a journal entry, you may want to further explore your topic by using other brainstorming exercises or even discussing it with your instructor and other classmates. Then you can revisit your topic in your journal.

## Cubing

Yet another way to generate ideas is by **cubing** your topic. Imagine a cube with six sides, or use a die from a game set you have around your house. Next, imagine the numbers for the commands given below are written on each side of the cube, or attach the commands to the sides of a die. Picture yourself rolling the cube (or roll the actual die), and write according to the commands that come up.

Listed below are the commands you should visualize on your cube.

1. **Describe it:** What does the subject look like? Sound like? Engage all five senses if possible.

2. **Compare and contrast it:** What is the subject similar to? What is it different from? How so?

3. **Free associate with it:** What does the subject remind you of? Any particular memories?

4. **Analyze it:** How does it work? What is its significance?

5. **Argue for or against it:** What advantages and disadvantages does it have?

6. **Apply it:** What are the uses of your subject? What can you do with it?

Write whatever comes to your mind for 10 minutes or so. When you have finished cubing, take the topics and subtopics you have generated and organize them by clustering or outlining them.

## Listing

Another way to brainstorm is to simply create a list of any ideas that pop into your head for about 10 minutes. After you have finished this listing, look for connections between ideas, or look for one main idea that encompasses several small ones.

Here is an example for the general topic of television:

| | |
|---|---|
| Entertaining | Usually 30-minute programs |
| Informative | Media |
| Corrupting | Listen |
| Poisoning | Corporate sponsorship |
| News | Music television |
| Comedy | Home shopping |
| Drama | "Boob tube" |
| Sports | Game shows |
| Educational | Remote control |
| Biased | Mind-numbing |
| Commercials | Weight gain |
| People | Dumbing down of society |

After examining the list, do you make any connections? Does anything stand out that you might want to write about? If so, try clustering or outlining the idea to see if it can be developed.

## Clustering or Mapping

Another technique you can use for brainstorming is **clustering**, sometimes referred to as mapping. You can cluster in two different ways:

- Start with possible topic ideas, then cluster them by drawing circles around them and connecting related ideas with lines.

- Start with a clustering grid, and then fill in the circles with ideas.

Whatever way you decide to cluster, start by putting a general topic in the middle of a blank page. If you want to use the first clustering method, jot down possible subtopics and details all around the central circle. After you have written down as many subtopics or details as you can, locate the more general subtopics, circle them, and attach these circles to the middle circle that holds the general topic. After this, find details that will support the subtopics, circle them, and attach these circles to the subtopic circles. When you have circled enough subtopics and details to start outlining or writing your paper, erase or cross out all the extra, unconnected information.

If you want to try the second clustering method, write your general topic in the middle of a blank page and draw lines from this circle to five or six circles (these will hold your subtopics). Then, draw lines from the subtopic circles to three or four other circles and fill them out (these will be your supporting details). Regardless of the clustering method you choose, you should allot at least 10 to 20 minutes for this brainstorming process. What you end up with might look something like the cluster/map shown in Figure 3.2, which uses non-conformists as the general topic.

Figure 3.2: **Example of a Cluster Map**

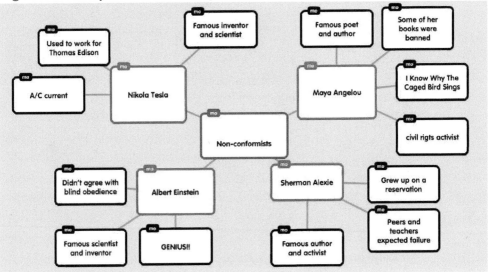

## Interviewing and Discussing

Often a topic or idea seems unclear at first. In this case, discussing the topic with others can facilitate clarification. Discussing your idea with or **interviewing** a classmate or a friend can offer a perspective that you had not thought of previously. Think of the subject as a friend or classmate asks questions that would naturally come up in conversation. Your "interviewer" might ask you what are termed *journalist questions*, such as the following:

|  |  |
|---|---|
| Who? | Who believes X? Who is involved? |
| When? | When did it happen? When did you change? |

| Why? | Why did X do Y? Why is this interesting? |
|------|------------------------------------------|
| What? | What happened? What did you do? |
| Where? | Where did it happen? Where were you? |
| How? | How did you become involved? How is it interesting? |

Make sure you listen to what you are saying as you are being "interviewed." Was there a particular part of the subject that you were most interested in talking about? If so, why? You may find that you have discussed your way into an interesting topic. If that does not prove fruitful, and you are still without a clear subject by the end of the "interview" session, change roles and ask your classmate or friend to respond to the questions.

## Questioning

If interviewing works best for you, but no one is available for interviewing. try **questioning** yourself about the subject. Think of your favorite attorney on television or in books. How would he or she cross-examine a witness? You should model your cross-examination of yourself in this manner. Below is a list of five categories to help you start narrowing your subject.

> **Definition**: How does the dictionary define the word or subject? How do most people define it? What is its history? Where did it come from? Give some examples.

> **Compare and contrast**: What is it similar to? What is it different than? Think also along the lines of synonyms (likes) and antonyms (opposites).

> **Relationship**: What are its causes and effects?

> **Circumstance**: Is it possible or impossible? When has it happened before? Are there any ways to prevent it?

> **Testimony**: What do people say about it? What has been written about it? Have you had any experience with it? Has any relevant research been done on the subject?

## Drawing or Creating Word Pictures

You could try brainstorming without words by sketching out your topic. What pictures do you immediately associate with your topic? Look at size, color, and juxtaposition of the pictures you sketch out or color in. What do these pictures and the way you sketch them tell you about your topic?

You can also try drawing a **word picture**. Begin by writing your topic in the center of the paper, drawing pictures and adding words. Consider this as freewriting with pictures—keep drawing until you find something in your images that you can use to narrow down your topic. Or you can create pictures just out of words that come to you as you think about your topic.

No matter which method of brainstorming you choose, the more you write, the more ideas you generate and the deeper you delve into the topic. If your brainstorming yields complex ideas, consider using more brainstorming methods to develop the ideas further. Moving beyond initial impressions and wrangling with contradictions are often the first step to writing an original and thought provoking essay.

## Writing a Thesis Statement
### (See Chapter 4.)

Many students find it challenging to write an effective **thesis statement**; the thesis statement is the most important part of the paper. A thesis statement should have two parts—your topic, and what you want to say about your topic. You may want to analyze a part of your topic, make an argument concerning it, or just simply show your readers a side of your topic that they may have not considered. Your purpose will vary depending upon the kind of essay you're writing. When writing your thesis statement, think about your audience. What do you want to show them? Why should it matter to them? What is the decorum of the situation?

During the drafting process, your thesis is not set in stone. In fact, you might consider it more of a "working" thesis. A working thesis identifies your initial purpose for writing, but may change as you write and discover new ideas.

## Outlining
### (See Chapter 6.)

**Outlining** can help you brainstorm for subtopics, or it can be used as a method for organizing the material that other brainstorming techniques have helped you generate. Either way, the value of the outline is its ability to help you plan, see logical connections between your ideas, and recognize obvious places to add new ideas and details.

An informal outline can be just a map of paragraphs you plan to use. Below is an example of an informal outline of an informative essay comparing the educational experiences of Sherman Alexie and Albert Einstein:

Thesis: Students who are non-conformists tend to develop critical thinking skills more easily

- Sherman Alexie was a non-conformist, and he refused to do as told—he succeeded, and became a famous author.

- Albert Einstein was also a non-conformist, and he chafed at expectations of absolute obedience in grade school.

- Conformity can limit a student's creativity and ability to think critically.

You can also add examples and supporting details to construct a more detailed informal outline.

The outline below is not a formal outline, which would have strictly parallel parts and would be expressed in complete sentences. Informal, or working, outlines help you get to the drafting stage, but they should not restrict you from changing subtopics or details to make your claim stronger.

I.  Introduction

    A.  Personal story about being a non-conformist in school

    B.  Thesis: Students who are non-conformists tend to develop critical thinking skills more easily.

III. Alexie

    A.  Alexie was a non-conformist, and he succeeded and became a famous author

    B.  Alexie was encouraged to do poorly by both peers and teachers

    C.  Alexie resisted this pressure and refused to do poorly

III. Einstein

    A.  Another non-conformist, Albert Einstein, when enrolled in elementary school, chafed at being expected to give total obedience

    B.  Later on, he took a personal course of study because his academic needs were not being met

    C.  Einstein became the most famous scientist of all time

IV. Conclusion

    A.  The point—conformity can limit a student's creativity and ability to think critically

B.   Some students who are non-conformists develop a critical consciousness that helps them succeed both in school and in life

C.   End with same or similar personal examples as in the intro.

## Composing the First Draft

The next step in the Writing Process is to take the ideas that you have generated through brainstorming and organize them into a preliminary order for your **first (or rough) draft**. At this time, you should decide on a specific thesis, a supporting organizational pattern, and details from your brainstorming. As you compose your first draft, you may find that you are missing enough supporting details or that you are unable to support your thesis effectively. Remember that writing is a process, and it may be time to return to one or more brainstorming activities to help narrow down your topic, which could reveal more supporting details.

The goal of the first draft is to get your ideas from your brain to the page. Your first draft may not be perfect. As Anne Lamott shares, "The only way I can get anything written at all is to write really, really shitty first drafts. The first draft is the child's draft, where you let it all pour out and then let it romp all over the place, knowing that no one is going to see it and that you can shape it later" (125). Rather than wrangling over an individual sentence, focus on the big picture. Tackle the process, and your topic, one paragraph, page, or point at a time. If you find yourself stuck at a particular point, move on to a different part of the essay. Once you've completed your rough draft, you can shape and clarify your ideas during the revision process.

Remember that the writing process never begins with the opening paragraph and never ends with the final punctuation mark. Also, it is best to begin writing as soon as a paper is assigned. This does not mean that you must work on the paper exclusively. By getting started early, you allow yourself time to ponder your idea, exhaust all possible angles, write, live your life, rewrite, focus on other things, and have someone else look over your essay before you revise it once again. Chapters 9 and 12 can help you with these later steps in the Writing Process.

# Chapter 4

# Thesis Statements

A thesis statement is, in many ways, the most important sentence in academic writing. A thesis may be a sentence or a series of sentences, but it is always at the heart of any piece of writing. If a reader cannot identify your thesis, the purpose of your text is not clear. Though many authors imply rather than clearly state their thesis statements, college essays typically require a clearly stated thesis in the paper's introduction. Think of your thesis statement as a declaration. The thesis statement marks the moment you step into the academic conversation and proclaim: this is why I am writing, and this is why it matters.

## Ingredients of an Effective Thesis Statement

1.  **Clarifies the subject of your paper:**
    A thesis is a summary of your paper. You will find that, sometimes, you begin your paper with one idea, but by the time you finish, your idea changes. This is a normal part of the writing process. Often, ideas are generated in the process of writing—ideas that don't get fully developed until writing begins. It's a good idea to think of your initial thesis statement as your working thesis; this will help you remember to go back and review it to ensure it matches  the message of your paper. Just remember to go back and change it!

2.  **Matters to the audience:**
    A thesis should be applicable to a larger audience outside of the classroom. Your instructor may give you guidelines concerning your audience, but even if he or she doesn't, a general academic audience is assumed for most academic essays. When writing your thesis statement, think about how another student in an unrelated  class would react to it. Would that student say, "So what? How does this apply to my life?" Your goal as a writer is to write a thesis statement that answers the questions "So what?" or "Who cares?"

3. **Interests the readers and gets their attention:**
   This is much like the connection with the audience; however, most topics will not be interesting to a wide audience. With that said, unusual approaches often generate the most interest from any audience.

4. **Is clear and specific:**
   When drafting your thesis, use specific terms that communicate exactly what you want your audience to know about your topic. For example, saying that *Facebook* is good can have a variety of meanings. However, if you want to argue that social networking sites like *Facebook* offer great opportunities for people to network, which can help them on the job market, that is a very specific statement that can be supported with evidence. Avoid words that are overly general or subjective. (See Chapter 8.)

5. **Is provable and arguable:**
   When you write an essay, you will be proving your opinion to a larger audience, but not everything is provable. Statements that are based on personal tastes or beliefs or vague statements cannot be proven, for example. However, your thesis must do more than restate a fact. An effective thesis makes an **arguable** claim and then proceeds to prove that claim throughout the essay.

   > Not Provable: *Harry Potter and the Sorcerer's Stone* is my favorite book.

   > Fact: In *Harry Potter and the Sorcerer's Stone*, Harry Potter thwarts Voldemort with help from his friends.

   > Claim: Harry Potter's journey from lonely boy below the stairs to Hogwarts hero resonates with young readers struggling to find their social identity.

A thesis identifies the central message of a paper. It acknowledges a writer's unique perspective on the topic. Furthermore, it acknowledges readers by engaging their interest and providing an overview of the essay.

Table 4.1: **How <u>Not</u> To Write A Thesis Statement**

| | |
|---|---|
| My home town is very important to me. | • Doesn't matter to the audience<br>• Doesn't get the reader's attention |

| There are a lot of fun things to do at the lake. | • Doesn't matter to the audience<br>• Doesn't get the reader's attention<br>• Isn't clear or specific |
|---|---|
| Taylor Swift is the best contemporary singer. | • Not provable |
| My father made me the person I am today. | • Doesn't matter to the audience<br>• Doesn't get the reader's attention<br>• Isn't clear or specific |
| My moral values are a big part of who I am. | • Doesn't matter to the audience<br>• Doesn't get the reader's attention<br>• Isn't clear or specific |
| The media sometimes has a positive effect on people and sometimes has a negative effect. | • Doesn't matter to the audience<br>• Doesn't get the reader's attention<br>• Isn't clear or specific<br>• Not provable |

## Kinds of Thesis Statements

Since a thesis statement reflects both the purpose and type of writing required, you must determine the context for your writing: who is your audience, what is your purpose, and what special circumstances are there (if any)? Then you write a working thesis that makes a tentative assertion or claim about your topic. If you are writing a research paper about the advantages and disadvantages of biodiesel fuel, your claim will be stated differently depending on whether your audience is an English class or a chemistry class. In the latter, you might choose to use technical language that would be unfamiliar to the former. The decorum of the situation will help you decide the proper approach.

As stated in Chapter 2, there are three main kinds of academic writing: expressive, informative, and persuasive. Each kind of writing focuses on different parts of the rhetorical triangle, and the style of each kind of writing is different; naturally, the thesis statement for each type of essay will be different as well.

**Expressive essays** are focused on the author. A thesis statement for an expressive essay typically does not make as strong of an argument as one for a persuasive essay. However, this doesn't mean that you should ignore the audience. Expressive thesis statements should still have a "So what?" Think about parts of your own life that are universal, and ask yourself the question: "What have I learned that can help the readers with their own lives?"

**Informative essays** focus on the subject, so they are not as personal as expressive essays. In many cases, informative essays focus on analyzing a subject in detail. Your goal is to ask your audience to look at your subject more closely or in a different way. When you **analyze**, you break down an issue or an idea into its component parts, evaluate the issue or idea, and present this breakdown and evaluation to your audience. When writing a thesis statement for an informative essay, you must explain what you are analyzing and introduce your interpretation based on that analysis.

**Persuasive essays** focus on the audience, and the goal of a persuasive essay is to convince the readers to either change their views or reconsider a view to which they did not subscribe. An effective persuasive thesis statement will follow all of the guidelines listed above, but will take an especially strong stand while taking the audience's opinions into consideration.

---

### Assignment 4.1

#### Evaluate Thesis Statements

Below are thesis statements written for an expressive essay. Evaluate each one using the criteria for effective thesis statements discussed earlier in this chapter. Which thesis statement(s) are the most effective and why? What makes the others ineffective?

- Hawaii is a great place to go on vacation.
- Watching my mother cope with the hardships of her life helped prepare me to face my own problems courageously.
- My father had a big influence on my life.
- My grandmother's strength influenced me and helped me become a strong individual.
- When we went to the Rocky Mountains, there was always something to keep us occupied.
- The volcanos in Hawaii are beautiful.

- In this paper, I'm going to talk about my family's vacation, explain what we did each day, and talk about how much fun we had as a family.

- A good friend is hard to find.

- My doll, even though it's broken, is my most cherished possession.

## Assignment 4.2
### Create Thesis Statements

Choose a pair of essays you have read or are reading for class.

After reading the essays, take 5 minutes to write about a common theme you detect in the readings.

In a small group, compare your notes. Work together to write a thesis statement that makes a compelling claim about the two essays.

After you have composed your group's thesis, choose one member of the group to write your thesis on the board.

As a class, assess the thesis statements using the criteria for effective thesis statements.

# Chapter 5

# Organization

> "One day Alice came to a fork in the road and saw a Cheshire cat in a tree: 'Which road should I take?' she asked. 'Where do you want to go?' was his response. 'I don't know,' Alice answered. 'Then,' said the cat, 'it doesn't matter.'"
>
> —Lewis Carroll

As writers, we know what we are trying to say. We understand the progression of our own thoughts and the connections between our ideas. However, these connections may be unclear to readers and the "natural" progression of our thoughts may seem confusing to another person. In addition, writing can feel overwhelming when you're in the middle of it. Organizing effective paragraphs around one topic or subtopic can help you keep your ideas straight as you write.

Effective writers apply **patterns of organization** to their ideas to help readers understand their message. You can think of organization like a roadmap or signs posted along the road to help readers reach their destination. It may be helpful to construct an outline of your writing first, then develop the main points and subpoints into paragraphs.

In addition, decorum is still an important consideration: Who is your audience? What do they value in a written message? How can you structure your essay to meet their values and expectations? How can organization clarify your logic?

## Patterns of Organization

On a smaller scale, patterns of organization are common strategies that writers use to organize and structure their writing. The human brain is hard-wired to pick up patterns, so once your reader notices you are using a particular pattern, they have a better idea of what to expect. Patterns of organization function as planned routes that guide readers through an essay. Below are some common patterns and ways to use them.

## Chronological organization

A chronology is an order of events. With this pattern, you move through events as they happen in real time, from the earliest event to the last. This is an ideal strategy for narratives, cause-and-effect essays, or any situation that depends on a clear sequence of events.

## Spatial organization

With spatial organization, you move visually through a space. Think of it like walking into a room. Your eyes naturally scan the space from left to right and top to bottom. This is an ideal strategy for descriptive writing or any situation where you are observing and describing things in a physical space. Spatial organization is also useful when describing movement.

## Climactic organization

While chronological and spatial organizational patterns are ideal for physical situations, climactic organization (also called order-of-importance) focuses more on ideas. This pattern is useful for managing a number of individual points or ideas you need to communicate to your audience. Organize your points in ascending order of importance, so the least important points appear at the beginning of your essay, and the most important points appear at the end. This pattern of organization is effective for persuasive and argumentative essays because you conclude with your most compelling point or piece of evidence.

## Compare and Contrast

This pattern is helpful when you are dealing with two ideas, events, or people. It allows you to describe similarities and differences between your two subjects. Compare and contrast can use a **point-by-point** organizational pattern. With this type of organization, you alternate between your two subjects. For example, you might write an essay comparing and contrasting two historical figures. Your first point may be your subjects' childhoods; your first paragraph would describe the childhood of the first person, and your second paragraph would describe the childhood of the second person. If your second point is political accomplishments, you would write a third paragraph about the first person's political accomplishments, and then a fourth paragraph about the second person's political accomplishments. If you make a point about one subject, you must make a parallel point about the second subject, even if it is just to note the absence of a particular point. After all, the absence can be as important as the presence of something, especially if you consider why it is not there. Another option for organizing compare-and-contrast is **subject by subject**. Instead of alternating from point to point (childhood, political accomplishments), you explore all the points about one subject (a historical figure), and then move on to the other.

## Simple-to-Complex organization

When dealing with complicated ideas, it is often useful to begin with simple concepts and progress toward more complex concepts. This pattern of organization often begins by providing context or background information that helps readers understand your later points. A **simple-to-complex** organizational pattern allows you to build on each piece of information as it is presented.

# Choosing and Combining Patterns of Organization

As noted above, certain types of writing lend themselves to various patterns of organization. However, patterns of organization can depend on your purpose and style as well. Imagine you've been assigned an expressive essay. You decide to write about the park where you played as a child. You could use a chronological pattern of organization to describe a single day in the park from morning to night. You could also use a chronological pattern to describe how the park changed over the years. Alternatively, you could use comparison and contrast to compare the park when you were a child to the park now. Though both approaches describe change, chronological organization shows the change as gradual over a length of time. Comparison and contrast might highlight your sense of loss as you juxtapose a description of a beautiful oak tree with the stump that stands there now. You could even organize your description of the park spatially and move from one area to the next. Choose the pattern of organization that supports the essay's purpose.

In addition, while many essays are structured around a single pattern of organization, complex writing assignments may warrant a combination of patterns. For example, in an essay describing the effects of the Great Recession of 2008, you could pick three aspects of the economic collapse as the main points of your essay and organize them in order of importance:

the stock market, housing, and unemployment. However, within each point, you could trace the effects of each problem chronologically.

The bottom line is that readers are lazy, and you don't want to make them work too hard. As William Zinsser points out, "the man snoozing in his chair with an unfinished magazine in his lap is a man who was given too much unnecessary trouble by the writer" (130). Clarifying the relationships between your ideas through a clear organizational pattern takes that burden from your reader.

### Assignment 5.1

### Practice Organization

Select an essay from the readings at the back of this book. Read through the essay carefully, noting the topic of each paragraph. After you have finished reading, create an outline of the essay. Include the thesis statement, topic of each paragraph, and the supporting evidence used to develop each paragraph. Here is an example using "Superman and Me."

Once your outline is complete, decide what pattern of organization the author used. How does this pattern of organization support the author's purpose?

Thesis: Reading saved Sherman Alexie's life, and he hopes to save the lives of Native American children in the same way.

1. Introduction
   a. The Superman comic
   b. Author's background/context
2. How he grew to love reading
   a. Alexie's father loved books
   b. Alexie loved his father
   c. He discovers the purpose of a paragraph
   d. He applies that knowledge to the Superman comic and learns to read
3. The effects of Alexie's love of reading
   a. Indian children are not expected to do well in school
   b. By reading, Alexie broke the stereotype of the uneducated Indian

4. Alexie decided he would not fail

    a. He read everything

    b. Now, he visits schools and teaches creative writing

5. Conclusion

    a. He is saving Native American children's lives

## Assignment 5.2

### Cut Up an Essay

After writing an essay, it can sometimes be difficult to imagine organizing it in any different way. After all, you've arranged your ideas and written your transitions to create a specific progression. The following activity encourages you and your classmates to experiment with different patterns of organization.

- Print a copy of an essay you've written recently. It can be a rough or final draft.

- Cut your essay into pieces so each paragraph is on a separate piece of paper. On the back of each paragraph, write the original paragraph number.

- Shuffle your paragraphs, and then have a classmate reassemble the essay.

- Compare your original paragraph order with your classmate's organization. Ask your classmate to explain his or her reasoning. If your classmate struggled to reassemble the essay, you most likely need to revise. Alternatively, your classmate's re-organization may suggest an alternative pattern of organization.

- You can repeat this exercise multiple times by adding transitions and re-organizing your essay before cutting it up and giving it to another classmate.

## Assignment 5.3

### Write an Op-Ed

This assignment asks you to write an op-ed piece suitable for submission to a major newspaper or other media outlet. For this assignment, you need to do the following:

1. Read op-eds that appear in the major regional newspaper or other media outlet for your city, such as the *The Muleskinner, The Warrensburg Daily Star-Journal, The Kansas City Star,* or *The St. Louis Post Dispatch*. Read several op-eds to get a sense of the topics and style of the articles that the newspaper or other media outlet prints.

2. Choose a topic that is timely and of interest to the readers of the publication that you choose.

3. The length and structure of your op-ed should follow the pattern of pieces recently published in your publication.

4. Keep your audience in mind—the readers of the publication.

5. Follow the basic op-ed pattern of organization, recommended by the Op-Ed Project, reprinted below.

### Tips for Op-Ed Writing from the Op-Ed Project
(*Note*: These are not rules; they are suggestions for approaching the project.)

**Lede** (a hook to catch the reader's attention)

**Thesis** (statement of argument)

**Argument** (based on evidence, such as stats, news, reports from credible organizations, expert quotes, scholarship, history, and firsthand experience. Use a mixture of developmental strategies to build your argument)

**Counter-claim** (in which you preempt your potential critics by acknowledging any flaws in your argument and address any obvious counter-claims)

**Conclusion** (often circling back to your lede)

# Chapter 6

# Body Paragraphs

A typical **body paragraph** in any essay is made up of a topic sentence, subtopics, and various levels of specific examples. The **topic sentence** functions in the paragraph just as the thesis statement functions in the essay. That is, the topic sentence tells the reader what the paragraph will be about just as the thesis statement tells the reader what the entire essay will be about.

The topic sentence also supports the thesis statement by offering a main point in the discussion. Likewise, each subtopic heading (refer to the outline example in Chapter 5) will support the specific focus of the paragraph.

Finally, the examples under each subtopic heading offer illustrations that support the assertions of the subheading. Thus, in a well-organized paragraph, the relationship of every detail to the topic sentence is obvious, and, in turn, the connection with the thesis is obvious.

Practicing and mastering the principles of paragraph form offers greater assurance toward mastering the essay. This mastery involves being familiar with unity, development, coherence and continuity within the paragraph and within the essay as a whole.

## Paragraph Unity

For a paragraph to have **unity**, each sentence in a body paragraph must directly relate to the purpose indicated in the topic sentence. The paragraph must come together as a whole to create a single expression of meaning that directly connects to the overall purpose of the essay. Any departure from the single purpose of the paragraph violates paragraph unity.

For example, if you were to bring into a paragraph about good teachers the idea that teachers' salaries need to be raised, you would be shifting the focus away from the main idea (good teachers); you would be breaking the unity in the paragraph. Stick to your topic sentence! Keep in mind that a paragraph is, by definition, a unified statement of a particular idea.

One way to test paragraph unity is to try to link each sentence in the paragraph to a word or phrase in the topic sentence. Draw lines and arrows if you must. Any sentence that you cannot obviously link to the topic sentence is probably irrelevant and, therefore, will undermine the effectiveness of your paper. This means you should revise the paragraph to maintain a sense of unity.

Another way to test the unity of a paragraph is to turn the topic sentence into a question. If the paragraph answers the topic sentence question, then you have a unified paragraph. If the paragraph does not answer the topic sentence question, then it's time to revise.

## Paragraph Development

Just because you make the claim that good teachers do not lecture in their classes in your topic sentence, your readers will not necessarily accept your viewpoint automatically. You must convince your audience that what you have to say is sound, sensible, and well-supported. You must explore your main idea explicitly, concretely, and thoroughly, and you must strive to include enough supporting evidence in each paragraph to present your point convincingly. Supporting evidence or examples can come from your own experiences, from hypothetical examples, research material, authoritative evidence, facts, or from just about any sound, reliable source.

Inadequate paragraph development is a serious weakness of beginning writers. No matter how organized and unified your ideas are, if they are not developed fully, you will have failed to communicate your message.

Many students ask, "What is enough support?" The answer is not concrete, but some general guidelines apply. You want enough support to convince your audience of the validity of your argument. For example, whose opinion is more likely to be accepted in a court of law: the defense attorney's claim that her client is innocent because the defendant's family and friends know he is innocent, or the prosecuting attorney's claim that the defendant is guilty because of fourteen eyewitnesses and extensive forensic evidence? Most readers would agree that the prosecuting attorney's claim has more factual support, which makes it appear more valid.

Valid evidence is convincing and supports opinions and observations. The same is true of paragraph development. You must provide enough information to convince your audience of the soundness of your argument. The average length of a paragraph in a college-level essay might run approximately three-fourths of a typed page or no fewer than four sentences. However, don't forget that quality is more important than quantity; it's much more impactful to have several carefully-crafted, thoroughly-developed paragraphs than it is to have a multitude of hastily crafted, underdeveloped paragraphs.

In moving from topic sentence to supporting evidence in a paragraph, you are moving from general to specific before broadening your focus at the end. Sometimes this technique is referred to as an hourglass because, like the shape of an hourglass, the information in your paragraphs moves from general, to specific, and back to general. The order and progression of this movement is essential to effective paragraphs, and an outline is the most efficient method of making certain this progression occurs logically.

The following is a paragraph from the essay mentioned in Assignment 5.1, about Sherman Alexie's short story "Superman and Me."

**Table 6.1: Levels of Development**

| | | |
|---|---|---|
| Students who are non-conformists tend to develop critical thinking skills more easily. | Thesis | Level I |
| Alexie was a non-conformist; he succeeded, and he became a famous author. | Topic Sentence (general statement that supports the thesis, but needs to be proved) | Level I |
| Alexie was encouraged to do poorly by both peers and teachers; if he had listened to them, he would not have succeeded. | Support (more specific) | Level II |
| Alexie resisted this pressure and refused to do poorly. | Support (even more specific) | Level III |
| Alexie read everything he could, he spoke up (instead of being quiet in class like his classmates), and he "refused to fail" (Alexie #). | Support (very specific) | Level IV |

| Alexie's actions show that he is a non-conformist; this, combined with the critical thinking skills he developed as an avid reader, likely led to his success as an author. | Connection to thesis | Level I |
|---|---|---|

These different levels highlight the arrangement of ideas in the paragraph, from general statement to specific examples. Always develop your ideas in the outline of your paragraph at least to the very specific (Level IV). The logic behind this recommendation is that you will most likely have to reach Level III (even more specific) before you can provide examples that are specific and concrete enough to persuade your readers of your general assertion (Level I).

In addition, the ideal number of Level II or Level III statements is three. If you offer only two examples, you could risk sounding dogmatic and inflexible. Four or more examples under the same subtopic, however, suggest you wish to appeal emotionally to your readers. Some readers might cry out, "Enough already!" There is such a thing as overkill; especially if your examples tend to be repetitive. You will not always be able to provide three examples, but that is a good goal to reach towards. Make sure you understand and can recognize the different levels of development so you can create effective outlines and, consequently, effective paragraphs.

When composing your essay, you have many different strategies of development available to you. You may write entire essays where the sole strategy is argumentation or comparison and contrast, but more often, you will combine many of these different strategies while writing an essay.

For example, a teacher may assign an argumentative essay on how secondary education can be improved, but you could incorporate narration to describe the ideal classroom. Then you could use comparison and contrast to reveal the differences between the ideal classroom and the typical classroom. Finally, you might discuss an opposing point of view (counter-claim) in order to disprove it.

The following list outlines some common strategies for supporting claims and developing paragraphs.

## Strategies 6.1
### Developing a Paragraph

*Analysis* breaks a complex concept, issue, book, film, or other object into smaller pieces, and then makes a conclusion about how the whole concept "works" based on a careful investigation of the individual elements.

*Argumentation* involves taking a strong stand on an issue supported by logical reasons and evidence intended to change a reader's mind on an issue or open a reader's eyes to a problem.

*Cause and effect* explains a cause and subsequent effects, or consequences, of a specific action, or it seeks to explain the causes of a specific circumstance (effect).

*Classification* entails dividing and grouping things into logical categories in order to see similarities, differences, and intersections between ideas and/or topics.

*Comparison and contrast* examines the similarities and differences between two or more things.

*Counter-claims* introduce opposing arguments. By introducing the reasons people might disagree with or object to your ideas, you demonstrate your understanding of the rhetorical situation. Revealing counter-claims also allows you to address or disprove these objections.

*Definition* employs an explanation of the specific meaning of a word, phrase, or idea.

*Description* uses vivid sensory details to present a picture or an image to the reader.

*Exemplification* makes use of many specific examples to explain, define, or analyze something.

*Narration* uses a story or vignette to illustrate a specific point or examine an issue.

| Assignment 6.1 |
| --- |
| **Develop a Paragraph 3 Ways** |
| • Chose a topic and develop a claim for the essay you are currently working on. Write one topic sentence that relates to your claim. |
| • Select 3 strategies of development from Strategies 6.1. |
| • Using the same topic sentence for each paragraph, write three paragraphs that develop your claim using a different strategy of development for each paragraph. |
| • Conclude each paragraph with a "clincher" that reiterates the main idea of your paragraph (See page 61 for further explanation). |
| • After you've completed your paragraphs, discuss your work with your classmates. Decide which developmental strategy works best for each topic. |

## Paragraph Coherence and Continuity

**Continuity** means literally "holding together." It is achieved through good organization and unity, and also by the language you use to illustrate to your readers how your ideas fit together. You can achieve **coherence** through the language you use. It will serve as transitions or devices that link sentences to each other. **Transitions** are also used to connect paragraphs, which link your ideas together in a smooth, logical order.

Transitions function like road signs. They alert readers to changes in topic and help identify important ideas. As a result, transitions serve both a functional and a stylistic purpose in an essay. On a functional level, transitions help keep your reader from being confused. They signal changes in topics and explain relationships between ideas. Stylistically, they create flow and make your writing more polished and professional. Transitional devices include pronouns and **demonstrative adjectives**, repetition of key words, the use of synonyms, transitional expressions, and **parallel construction**.

The following list outlines these common strategies for increasing continuity and working on transitions within and between paragraphs.

When you start working with transitions, it is easy to fall into a habit of using the same transition over and over again. When you edit your paper, circle the transitions. If you notice you are using the same one too much, pull out a thesaurus to find a suitable replacement. Consult Table 6.2 or a thesaurus for additional help.

## Strategies 6.2
### Creating Continuity and Using Transitions

*Pronouns and demonstrative adjectives*—When their antecedents are clearly understood, pronouns (they, it, she, he) help the reader recognize that the phrase or sentence in which they appear is linked to the preceding idea. For example: "Steinbeck the biologist is interested in 'the animal motivation underlying human conduct.' Frequently in his fiction he equates human and animal conduct … . This close association between human and animal life leads to the extensive use of animal imagery and symbolism in his fiction" (Heitkamp 63).

Demonstrative adjectives (that, this, these, those) also clearly link the sentence containing them with the preceding sentences. Notice how the demonstrative adjective links the following two sentences: "Recognition of the unity of all life is the basis for John Steinbeck's artistic use of nature. One of the major expressions of this unity is the kinship that man feels with the land" (Heitkamp 6).

*Parallel construction*—This transitional device links your sentences and ideas by repeating a grammatical structure, thereby forcing your audience not only to keep the focus in mind but to realize the connection between your ideas.

Note, for example, President Lincoln's use of parallel construction in his famous "Gettysburg Address" and the power of its connected ideas to hold his audience:

> It is rather for us to be here dedicated to the great task remaining before us; that from these honored dead we take increased devotion to that cause for which they gave the last full measure of devotion; that we here highly resolve that these dead shall not have died in vain; that this nation, under God, shall have a new birth of freedom; and that government of the people, by the people, for the people, shall not perish from the earth.

Without the parallel construction, the impact of President Lincoln's speech may not have been as long-lasting.

*Repetition of key words and use of synonyms*—The important rule here is to repeat key words, or those words that help keep the essay's purpose in the minds of your audience. Notice how the words "dead" and "the people" are repeated in the example above.

Be careful, however, that you do not rely too heavily on this transitional technique; too much repetition becomes monotonous. If you feel you are repeating the same word too often, substitute a synonym. For instance, in the previously mentioned example, Lincoln could have said "fallen" or "departed" if he was concerned about being overly repetitive.

*Transitional expressions*—Each of these words has a definite function, whether it is to show logical order or to indicate logical relationships between ideas and sentences. Without these **transitional expressions**, your sentences would make little sense and certainly would not fit together to develop your idea, see Table 6.2.

A word of caution, however: be sure the transitional expression you choose does precisely what you want it to do. Do not simply close your eyes and select a phrase from the list. Use an appropriate term for the meaning or connection you wish to convey. Never use "furthermore" when "however" is what you need to alter the direction or to qualify a statement.

**Table 6.2: Transitional Expressions**

| | |
|---|---|
| **Addition** | moreover, furthermore, besides, likewise, also, too, finally, second, third, last, additionally |
| **Cause** | since, because |
| **Comparison** | similarly, likewise |
| **Concession** | although, though, despite |
| **Condition** | unless, provided that, if |
| **Contrast** | but, yet, however, nevertheless, in contrast, on the contrary, nonetheless, whereas, even though, although, otherwise, on the other hand |
| **Exception** | except |
| **Exemplification** | for example, for instance |

| Intensification | indeed, in fact |
|---|---|
| Place | where, here, near, beyond |
| Purpose | (in order) to, to this end |
| Repetition | in other words, as I have said, as previously mentioned, as stated above |
| Result | therefore, thus, consequently, as a result, hence |
| Summary | in conclusion, in short, all in all, overall, finally |
| Time | when, after, before, until, as long as, meanwhile, while, immediately, soon, afterward, then, henceforth |

### Assignment 6.2

#### Find Transitions

Using Sherman Alexie's essay in the back of the book, highlight or underline the transitions he uses.

## Transitions Between Paragraphs

One of the trickiest transitions can be the move from one paragraph to another. Many emerging writers attempt to create a connection by introducing the new topic in the final sentence of the old paragraph. However, this transition violates the principal of unity. Recall that a unified body paragraph focuses on one specific topic identified in a topic sentence. When you drop a new topic in at the end of a paragraph, it often surprises or confuses the reader. A more effective strategy is the **hinge sentence**. A hinge sentence appears at the beginning of the new paragraph and might even serve as your topic sentence. It begins with a reference to the topic of the previous paragraph, and then introduces the new topic.

For example, in "Is Google Making Us Stupid," Nicholas Carr writes:

> . . . In Google's world, the world we enter when we go online, there's little place for the fuzziness of contemplation. Ambiguity is not an opening for insight but a bug to be fixed. The human brain is just an outdated computer that needs a faster processor and a bigger hard drive.

> The idea that our minds should operate as high-speed data-processing machines is not only built into the workings of the Internet, it is the network's reigning business model as well. The faster we surf across the web—the more links we click and pages we view—the more opportunities Google and other companies gain to collect information about us and to feed us advertisements. (149)

The last portion of the first paragraph discusses how, on the internet, the "fuzziness of contemplation" is exchanged for machine-like efficiency. The first portion of the second paragraph addresses how internet companies profit from this tendency. As you can see, the transitional sentence links these topics.

Carr also uses the synonymous key words "processor," "hard drive," and "machines" to create unity through repetition of technological terms. He uses the transitional expressions "not only" and "as well" to show that he is building on a previously introduced idea.

All transitions assist you, the writer, in avoiding dull repetition by making the expression of your ideas more interesting and more varied. These devices keep your reader from having to leap from one idea to another because they offer convenient and persuasive bridges, which add to the effect of your essay. Most writers find that they naturally include the transitional devices both within and between paragraphs, but additional editing might be required during the revision process to ensure that there is adequate bridging.

## Assignment 6.3
### Workshop a Body Paragraph

- Print out one body paragraph from the essay you are currently working on.

- Underline the Topic Sentence.

- Using arrows, link the other sentences in your paragraph to a word or phrase in the topic sentence.

- Next to each sentence, label its specificity according to the chart on page 53–54.

- Underneath your paragraph, answer to the following question:

- How could your paragraph be improved? (Does your paragraph need work in terms of unity, development, coherence?)

# Wrapping Up the Paragraph

Finally, if your paragraph is a long one, you might consider including a summary sentence, a **clincher**, to close your paragraph. The inclusion of such a sentence serves at least two purposes. First, it brings closure to the main idea of the paragraph, especially if you have provided extensive examples. Closure helps your audience by returning them to your central idea and reminding them of your specific intention in the paragraph.

Second, the summary sentence is on the same level of generality as your topic sentence; therefore, it will make your task of bridging the connection between this paragraph and the next easier than it would be if you had to move from a very specific level of generality, a minor support statement, to a new topic sentence in a new paragraph. This final summary sentence clinches the discussion and emphasizes the main idea.

# Chapter 7

# Introductions and Conclusions

The **introduction** to your essay is an invitation to the reader. If your invitation is boring, they won't join you. After all, there are plenty of other interesting materials to read. In addition to capturing interest, the introductory paragraph also makes a commitment to readers. It identifies the topic, states the thesis, and previews the discussion that follows in the succeeding paragraphs. **Conclusions** are also important because they explain the essay's ideas in a larger context and underscore why the discussion was worthwhile. Contrary to what you may have been told, conclusions do not simply repeat all of your essay's main points.

The following student essay contains helpful insights on how to write an effective introduction.

---

### Student Essay, "How I Write an Introduction"

by Natalie Gorup

First impressions matter. This is perhaps one of the reasons writing introductions can be so difficult—we feel the pressure of wanting to make a good first impression on our readers, just as we feel the pressure of wanting to "impress" our classmates or co-workers the first time we meet them. But because they matter so much, introductions are worth the care and attention we give to any first meeting.

When you "meet" your reader in your introduction, be kind. Be empathetic enough to realize that s/he has probably just spent a busy day doing many other things before reading your writing. Help to draw your reader in by both catching his or her attention and helping him or her to gently "wade in" to what you will be talking about. (Cannonballs might be exciting, but they are also sometimes unpleasantly shocking!) I like to think of the opening scenes of films, which often use a long

---

shot, middle shot, close shot effect to situate their viewers and give them important information they might need for understanding the story that will follow.

But then comes the challenge of fitting these concerns to scale. When I scale my introductions, I generally try to picture a funnel: the funnel's wide mouth is the top of the paragraph, while the funnel's narrowest point, its thesis, often appears at the end of the introduction. I have to arrive at this narrowest point before I can continue on with my argument, but I will need to decide how steep the slide from the mouth of the funnel to its narrowest point needs to be. If I start too broadly, I will set myself the task of covering a great distance in just one short paragraph; if I start too narrowly, I'll find myself repeating various versions of my thesis for a whole paragraph, but with no needed context! Finding the Goldilocks "funnel" is the ideal: make some wider connection to the reader-of-the-wider-world and then "zoom in" as you help that reader focus on what you have to say—because, after all, you are going to spend the rest of your essay illustrating just how important what you have to say might be.

Introducing complex ideas is challenging, but when you "teach" your points gently to your readers, with the gradual slide down the funnel, you can sometimes get it "just right."

---

### Assignment 7.1

#### Create an Analogy

Natalie Gorup includes many analogies in her essay on introductions. She states that an introduction is like:

- A first impression

- A funnel

- Goldilocks finding the porridge, chair, and bed that are "just right"

- Wading into a pool gradually as opposed to a performing a cannonball

- A camera zoom technique, similar to the first shot in a movie that orients the viewer to the context

How else would you describe an introduction? Create your own analogy and explain it.

# Effective Introductions

It's imperative to capture the audience's attention with a **hook**. A hook is an interesting beginning. The first few sentences, in particular, "hook" the readers and make them want to continue reading. Writing an introduction can be difficult, especially writing one that doesn't sound too bland or cliché. Below are some strategies for writing introductions in ways that will interest your readers.

---

**Strategies 7.1**

### Writing Effective Introductions

**Intriguing Quotation:**

> Example: "Dave, stop. Stop, will you? Stop, Dave. Will you stop, Dave?" –*2001: A Space Odyssey*, used by Nicholas Carr

**Interesting fact or example:**

> Example: A survey by the National Center for Biotechnology Information concluded that the average person's attention span dropped from 12 seconds in 2000 to 8 seconds in 2013.

**Anecdote (relevant short story):**

> Example: "I learned to read with a Superman comic book." –Sherman Alexie

**Interesting, non-obvious question:**

> Example: "Is fiction good for us?" –Jonathan Gottschall

**Strongly stated opinion:**

> Example: "Now, even better news than that of short assignments is the idea of shitty first drafts." –Anne Lamott

**Vivid description:**

> Example: The bus accelerated gruffly, leaving behind a cloud of opaque smoke stretching toward the sky. The smoke's wispy fingers stretched higher, gradually overtaking the clear horizon.

**Intriguing statement:**

> Example: I've never been popular, in the traditional sense.

**Thoughtful comparison:**

> Example: The act of writing is like working out: the more you exercise the writing muscle, the stronger you become at writing.

**Assignment 7.2**

### Write Three Hooks

With a current writing project of your own, try developing at least three possible hooks from Strategies 7.1. Developing several hooks will enable you to see that there are a variety of options for how writers go about securing readers' interests.

Share your hooks with a peer, and ask them which one is most compelling. Which essay would they want to continue reading and why?

## Effective Conclusions

Since the words in the conclusion are literally the last words your audience reads, it is important to end on a high note. Toward the end of the essay, it is often easy to trail off into summary or hammer out a final rambling paragraph to meet the length requirements. A successful conclusion returns to the main ideas introduced in the essay, but avoids repeating what has already been said. You should be particularly concerned with helping the reader move back from the close details to the big picture so they understand the importance or significance of the essay.

The goal is to **synthesize** (make connections between your ideas) rather than **summarize** (restate your ideas). To this end, you might answer the question "so what?" In other words, now that you have presented your ideas, why should readers care? Why are these ideas important? Why do they matter? If the introduction is a funnel, narrowing to your argument, the conclusion is an inverted funnel, easing the reader back to the real world and the implications of your argument. You could discuss the wider implications of your ideas, propose a solution for any problems you addressed, or suggest your reader take action.

**Strategies 7.2**

### Writing Effective Conclusions

**Discuss the larger significance of your ideas:**

Example: "Remember this in moments of despair. If you find that writing is hard, it's because it is hard. It's one of the hardest things people do." -William Zinsser

Example: "I am smart. I am arrogant, I am lucky. I am trying to save our lives." –Sherman Alexie

**Proposal that calls the reader to action:**

>Example: Students shouldn't rely solely on their professors for their educational growth; instead, students should take action themselves. This means that they should read materials on their own, explore their campus community, and participate in discussions of critical issues.

**Quotation:**

>Example: Peter Elbow, an esteemed compositionist, says, "Meaning is not what you start with, but what you end up with."

**Anecdote:**

>Example: "So, of course, you can imagine my excitement when I received the good news: 'thanx so much for uhelp ican going to graduate now.'" -Ed Dante

**Vivid description:**

>Example: "A friend of mine suggests opening up the jar and shooting them all in the head. But I think he's a little angry, and I'm sure nothing like this would ever occur to you." -Anne Lamott

**Hook and Return:**

Return to the hook from your introduction, but with some variation to indicate the significance of the essay.

>Example: "I'm haunted by that scene in *2001*. . . . That's the essence of Kubrick's dark prophecy: as we come to rely on computers to mediate our understanding of the world, it our own intelligence that flattens into artificial intelligence." –Nicholas Carr

### Assignment 7.3
### Write an Effective Conclusion

Write a conclusion that could accompany the most effective introduction you wrote for Assignment 7.2. Be sure to revisit the strategy you chose for your introduction. For example, if you began with an anecdote, return to that anecdote, but from a new angle. If you began with a quotation, provide a deeper analysis of that quotation.

# When to Write Introductions and Conclusions

It is generally more productive to start with the body of the essay and write the introduction and conclusion last. After the essay is written, you know the essay's purpose and the main points you included. If you write these important paragraphs first, you may need to rewrite them since a paper's ideas can shift in the writing process.

Writing introductions can be a tricky process, but it is important to remember that words can be rewritten to complement your body paragraphs and conclusion. Introductions should be creative and capture the reader's interest, but they can be revised as you develop the body paragraphs of your essay. Just remember, it is important to make an attempt so you will have a draft to work with and revise.

An introduction isn't effective if it doesn't lead in to the main point of the essay, even if it captures the audience's attention well. Likewise, a conclusion isn't effective if it doesn't tell the readers why they should care about the discussion. Introductions and conclusions should be thoughtful, creative, and clear to support your thesis most effectively. The first and last impressions of your essay are both vitally important in shaping the readers' ideas.

# Chapter 8

# Style

> "Most of us find our own voices only after we've sounded like a lot of other people."
>
> —Neil Gaiman

When Franklin D. Roosevelt addressed a nation in the grip of the Great Depression, he famously declared, "The only thing we have to fear is fear itself—nameless, unreasoning, unjustified terror which paralyzes needed efforts to convert retreat into advance." Afterward a journalist observed, "Any man who can talk like that in times like these is worthy of every ounce of support a true American has." Though Roosevelt's New Deal remained controversial, his words resonated with the American people. We remember the words, "The only thing we have to fear is fear itself," long after the context and the rest of the speech are forgotten because they are powerful, compelling words. Thus, the **style** of a well-chosen word or a well-crafted sentence has the potential to evoke emotion, persuade a reluctant audience, and communicate a message more clearly and effectively.

## Tone

**Tone** describes the general attitude an author uses to address an audience. For example, an author may use an informal, conversational tone for a blog post on the importance of farmer's markets. She may describe a visit to a local market, lingering on descriptive details of friendly vendors and sun-kissed tomatoes. She may address her audience with an inclusive "we" or "us" because she assumes her readers share her concerns and experiences.

However, if she wrote a letter to the mayor advocating a tax break for farmers who sell locally, a formal tone would be more effective. Her essay would privilege facts over description and use concrete, business-like language to demonstrate the economic advantages of the tax break. The author would adapt her tone to meet the needs of the particular audience.

Tone is closely linked with decorum since the appropriate tone depends on context, audience, and genre. There are many types of tone: serious to humorous, logical to emotional, friendly to businesslike, or objective to subjective, to name a few.

---

**Assignment 8.1**

**Identify Tone**

Write a paragraph about how tone impacts the message of one of the sample student essays from the back of the textbook. Think about what kind of audience the student must have had in mind when using that tone.

In the first sentence, identify the tone, whether it was or was not effective, and highlight a main reason why. Then use the rest of your paragraph to develop that idea.

Use at least one piece of textual evidence, and an appropriate signal phrase.

---

## Voice

As tone relates to an author's audience, style relates to an author's voice. Style creates space for an author to incorporate his or her personality into the composition.

Though teachers usually provide guidelines for the appropriate voice and style for a specific assignment, effective essays are written by people—not robots. Incorporating moments of humor, drama, sarcasm, and suspense make writing more meaningful for both the author and the audience. All of these choices are examples of an author expressing his or her voice.

While voice is a personal expression, it is nonetheless connected with an author's rhetorical purpose. For example, the Chicana author Gloria Anzaldúa includes Spanish words and phrases in her writing to celebrate her culture and draw attention to the linguistic diversity of American readers. Likewise, if we hear a song by Kayne West, even if it's sung by a different person, we can recognize his personal style and voice in the words and cadence.

# Diction

**Diction** refers to an author's word choice. On one level, every word has a literal, **denotative** meaning. These meanings appear in tidy, alphabetized rows in the dictionary, but rhetoric reminds us that words can have different meanings or implications for different audiences.

Every word also carries a **connotation**. Every word is infused with associations and emotional overtones that the word acquires over time. For example, "home" carries associations of warmth, security, family, comfort, and affection for most people. The word "residence" objectively describes a place where someone lives, but it might also carries connotations of emptiness, temporariness, and business. "Residence" is a word in a rental contract; "home" is Dorothy's mantra in *The Wizard of Oz*.

Just as words have both connotations and denotations, words can also be divided between the **concrete** and **abstract**. Abstract words describe ideas, feelings, and other intangible concepts. Concrete language describes physical objects.

- Abstract: Love, wisdom, cowardice, beauty, fear, liberty.
- Concrete: sandpaper, soda, oak tree, smog, cow, rocking chair, pancake.

Writing that relies too heavily on abstract language can sound vague. Writing that never moves beyond concrete details can leave readers wondering why these objects matter or what they mean. Effective writing must combine concrete and abstract words. Often writers introduce an abstract concept and then illustrate that concept with concrete examples. Alternatively, a writer may begin with concrete description and then explain the significance in more abstract language.

# Vivid Language

Vivid writing replaces generic words with more descriptive language. Vivid language tends to be specific. Thus, a bird becomes a robin and a flower becomes a daffodil. Abstract words have more vivid synonyms as well. "Despondent" creates a more vivid image than "sad." Similarly, over-used abstractions can be replaced with less common words, and create more compelling alternatives.

**Table 8.1: Compare Word Choice**

| Generic Language | Vivid Language |
|---|---|
| blue | azure, cobalt, navy, sea blue, turquoise |
| car | Ford Escort, Toyota Camry, Volkswagen Beetle |
| friend | school acquaintance, close friend, movie pal |
| house | home, abode, igloo, apartment, student dormitories |
| hungry | famished, ravenous, starving |
| piece of literature | short story, poem, novel, play |
| river | Danube, Mississippi, Nile |
| the city | Austin, Los Angeles, Nashville, New York |
| The musician smiled at the audience. | The musician flashed a lop-sided grin as he slipped off stage. |
| Many single parents work hard to support their families. | After long shifts at thankless, minimum-wage jobs, many single parents return home exhausted. |
| The Mariana Trench is the lowest place on Earth. It is seven miles deep and home to small, aquatic creatures. | Seven miles below the surface, the Mariana Trench houses shrimp and sea cucumber that have adapted to a world without sunlight. |

## Sentence Fluency

The length and structure of sentences shape the tone and style of a piece of writing. Short sentences pop. They create energy. They create tension. They may use repetition to enhance a point. Alternatively, a writer may slow the pace down with a long, languid sentence that ambles across the page and asks the reader to reflect. As a writer, you have the power to explore different sentence lengths for different dramatic effects.

Varied sentence lengths and structures also help readers pick out important details. Readers typically look for important information at the beginnings and ends of sentences. Ideas buried in the middle of a long sentence may effectively disappear.

# Active Voice and Passive Voice

In an **active voice** sentence, the subject performs the action. For example, Sally kicked the ball. In contrast, in a **passive voice** sentence, the subject receives the action. Consider this example: The ball was kicked by Sally. Sentences written in the active voice tend to more concise and compelling because it is easier to visualize the action being performed by the subject of the sentence.

- Passive: The roof was torn off the barn by the wind.
- Active: The wind tore the roof off the barn.
- Passive: *Romeo and Juliet* was read by the freshman class.
- Active: The freshman class read *Romeo and Juliet*.

You can recognize sentences written in the passive voice because the verb will include a form of "to be" (am, is, was, were, are, been), and they will often include the phrase "by the." Not all sentences using a form of "to be" are passive. Sentences should be rewritten to describe the action more successfully.

- The zombies were marching toward Main Street.
- The zombies marched toward Main Street.
- *Pet Sematary* was written by Stephen King. He was inspired to write the novel while living alongside a busy highway.
- Stephen King wrote *Pet Sematary* while living alongside a busy highway.

## Assignment 8.2
### Show, Don't Tell

Re-write the following sentences to make them more interesting. Use vivid language and active verbs.

The dog was annoying.

I had a really bad nightmare.

A student's life is hard.

The movie was dull.

The class was boring.

The test was very difficult.

The fire alarm was loud.

After you've re-written the sentences, discuss your revisions with a group of your classmates. Select the most interesting revisions to share with the class.

## Assignment 8.3

### Create Vivid Language

Revise the following sentences to eliminate word choice problems and make them clear, concise, and vivid.

Example:

Original: In my opinion, the signs posted in my city should have reflective letters.

Corrected: The traffic signs in Warrensburg should have reflective letters.

1. There has been an accident at a corner near campus every day beyond a shadow of a doubt.

2. Fraught with tension, the room where the recent city manager's meeting was held felt like it was swimming with the sweat of all the attendees in the room.

3. I think the facts reveal that better signs are needed.

4. It is quite surprising that in this day and age more people do not protest the number of accidents that have occurred in our city each and every day.

5. We all hope that the city manager will come out of the apparent comatose state he is in and work on changing how the signs are made and posted.

## Assignment 8.4

### Compare Writing Styles

Read the essays by Nicholas Carr and Jonathan Gottschall that both describe the effects of media. As you read, note each author's style. List the stylistic choices the authors make. How do those choices reflect their purposes for writing? Which do you prefer? Why?

# Chapter 9

# Revising, Editing, and Proofreading

The first usage of the word *revise* is recorded in the *Oxford English Dictionary* as occurring in 1589. It literally meant "the fact of being seen again."

To **revise** means to read, review, and change with the aim of improving your writing. Basically, revising means changing your essay. Revising is the part of the writing process focused on the global characteristics of writing and those elements that contribute to the rhetorical situation, content, organization, or style. Remember, each draft of an essay is a step in the writing process, and each draft is a work in progress. It is always a good idea to write multiple drafts of an essay in order to produce a quality piece of writing that accurately reflects your abilities.

**Editing** and **proofreading** are additional, but essential, steps in the writing process. Many writers make the mistake of focusing on error correction and proofreading before taking the time to develop, clarify, and organize ideas fully through drafting and revision. Although the parts of the writing process are not finite and often overlap, editing and proofreading should be treated as activities separate from revision. These skills are designed to address what writing specialists call **local issues**, such as grammar, sentence variety, mechanics, spelling, and formatting.

As such, editing comes after you feel confident about the choices you have made in content, organization, and style. You might compare editing and proofreading to washing, waxing, and polishing your car. It would be absurd to take the time to do these things to a vehicle that does not run! Drafting and revising ensures that your writing is first fine-tuned. Then you edit to make it shine on the surface.

There are different levels of both revising and editing. **Global characteristics** of writing can be found on each different level within your essay. Be sure to revise and edit on all levels: the overall essay, the paragraphs, the sentences, and the words. It is best to divide these levels of revision or editing and work on them separately since a good writing plan involves an examination of all levels.

## Focus Primarily on Revision

Writers who revise often discover and develop new or better ideas about their writing style, their topic, or their essay during the revision process. Skilled writers view revision as a necessary part of their writing because it is useful for generating new ideas, focusing and reorganizing ideas, and polishing the overall paper.

You can add, delete, and substitute material during the revision process. For example, if a sentence is unclear, you can add information to clarify your point, delete unclear words or phrases, or substitute a new sentence that is makes more sense. Perhaps, during a secondary reading of your essay, you realize that your main point shifts halfway through; revision allows you to make sure your main point is consistent throughout the entire piece.

### Organization
*(See Chapter 5.)*

Focusing on organization means that you are checking to make sure that the main idea and supporting ideas clearly relate to your thesis and purpose. Good organization is the glue that holds the central message and all supporting content together. Examining the organization on its own helps you to see whether you have included all the important points or whether you have added something unrelated that needs to be removed. Sometimes, an outline is the best way to see whether or not everything in your essay relates back to the main idea or thesis.

### Content
*(See Chapters 4 and 6.)*

Focusing on content for revision purposes involves looking at the central message of your essay. Look at the big picture. What is your central message? Everything in your essay (from words to paragraphs to graphics) should revolve around this central idea. If everything does not connect to one main idea, you may need to revise your thesis statement or a paragraph's topic sentences. In addition, you should check to make sure that your content is original, and thoughtful, and fully developed.

## Style
### (See Chapter 8.)

Focusing on style allows you to examine whether the words and sentences are appropriate for your topic and your audience. Look at the formality of your language. Does it fit with your thesis, audience, and purpose? In other words, does it fit the decorum of your writing situation? If not, you may need to revise your word choices. As a writer, you want to choose your words and sentence patterns to fit both you and your audience. Although dressing up your essay with words you have found in the thesaurus may seem like a way to elevate your writing, the result will be pretentious and unnatural; this is a sure way to lose credibility.

## Rhetorical Situation or Context
### (See Chapter 10.)

Focusing on all of the elements of the rhetorical situation, or context will ensure you have a balanced essay. Especially at the revising stage, looking at how the audience will view your message in context will help you identify supporting evidence that does not fit or sentences that do not sound appropriate. If you are trying to persuade your audience of something, be sure to take the time to understand the detailed aspects of your audience. The interplay between audience and purpose is a delicate one; using an approach that will allow you to share your message in a way that is neither too strong nor too weak is an even greater balancing act.

## Strategies for Revising

"I'm not a very good writer, but I'm an excellent rewriter."

—James Michener

Consider the following strategies for effectively revising your writing. You will not use every strategy on every essay, and different types of assignments will require different methods. Revision is a part of the writing process that is unique to the writer, and knowing your writing strengths and weaknesses will help you decide which of these steps will help you improve your paper on the global level in regard to content, organization, and style. Also, your teacher will likely provide feedback and guidance on your writing. Try using one (or more) of these strategies to address your teacher's concerns.

## Read a Printed Copy

Although we live in a digital world, using a printed version of your writing for revision enables you to make quick notes in the margins of your essay as ideas occur to you. Hard copies are also easy to read and reduce any tendency you may have to edit your writing as you read.

Ideally, you will have written your draft well in advance of any deadline, and you will have given yourself a few days of rest before beginning the revision process. In this situation, reading will remind you of what you have written and allow you to see your draft with fresh eyes, which will help you catch issues you may have otherwise overlooked.

However, college life is often less than ideal, and you may find yourself moving immediately from drafting to revising. So, if you have just written your draft, why take the time to read it? Regardless of how clearly you outline, how logically you think, or how quickly you type, you must read your writing to discover areas that might be improved through revision.

## Annotate Your Draft

Circle, highlight, or note any issues that surface as you read. Perhaps a paragraph seems out of place or a sentence no longer makes sense. You may realize that your writing does not support your thesis, or you have strayed from your thesis statement completely. Maybe your enthusiasm for the topic has led you to include a few well-intentioned, but unrelated, rants. Whatever the concern, identify it through annotation and keep reading. You should not begin expanding, condensing, focusing, or opting for a different course of action until you have read completely through your draft and identified all areas that might benefit from revision.

## Read Your Essay Aloud

Read your essay aloud to a friend, and be sure to read exactly what you have written. As you read, use a highlighter to mark places where you stumble or think there is a problem. Ask a peer to use a marker on his or her copy of your essay, and then write question marks next to elements that do not make sense or need further clarification.

You can also have someone else read your paper to you. Be sure to adopt the role of the reader or audience as you listen, and use a marker to put checks or question marks next to words or sentences you want to review after the reader finishes your essay.

## Assess Your Essay

Answer questions like those listed in Strategies 9.1 to review your essay as though you were the reader or audience. As you answer the questions, highlight and annotate places in your essay that need improvement.

## Strategies 9.1

### Assessing Your Writing

1. What is the subject of this essay? How does it fit the assignment?

2. Who is the audience? What does the audience likely know about this subject? What are the expectations of the audience?

3. What is the purpose of the essay (to analyze, to inform, to entertain, to persuade)? List specific examples that help determine the purpose of the essay.

4. What is the thesis statement?

5. What are the supporting points for the thesis?

6. Does the essay seem to struggle in any areas? If so, where? If not, how can you tell?

7. What are the most effective parts of the essay?

8. Which parts of the essay still need the most work?

9. What questions or problems do you have about the essay?

## Create a Reverse Outline

An easy way to determine if you have organizational issues is to create a reverse outline. Instead of outlining what you intend to write, you can use a reverse outline to tell you what you have written in a very clear way; you can do this by using one short statement to describe the main point of each paragraph. Now you can quickly identify whether you may have omitted any important points, added unrelated information, or repeated yourself.

The reverse outline also works well when applied to paragraph organization. However, when working with paragraph organization, do not outline what each sentence says; instead, outline what each sentence does. For example, a reverse outline of the previous paragraph might look like this:

a. Introduces reverse outline

b. Explains reverse outline

c. Lists benefits of reverse outline

If you need to expand your details, condense or clarify your ideas, or rearrange your sentences, a reverse outline will help you determine where to start.

## Color-Code Your Draft

Use highlighters to clearly show the different parts of your essay. If you use one color for main points, one for transition statements, another for definitions, and still another for explanations or details, you will begin to recognize issues with organization, repetition, and balance.

This technique is particularly useful when writing compare/contrast essays, position papers, arguments, or when using source material. For example, when you color-code your writing in a compare/contrast essay, you should detect frequently alternating colors if you have used a point-by- point-organization, or you should detect large sections of each color if you have used a subject-by-subject arrangement. Highlighting sourced material used in any writing can help you recognize whether you have relied too heavily on the words of others; this method can also help you see when you have dropped information in without any explanation.

## Cut Up Your Draft

A great way to check transitions and the organization of an essay is to cut it into pieces, literally. When each paragraph becomes a separate piece, you can both discover overlooked problems and play with the arrangement of your essay. If you are unable to reassemble it, then revise transitions or the organization to help put the essay back together more easily.

For an even more revealing exercise, you might have a friend attempt the reconstruction. If he or she is unable to put your essay back in order, it is time to revise.

## Create a Paragraph Essay

You can check the coherence of an essay and your organization by creating a paragraph essay. To begin, simply create a paragraph by copying your thesis statement and each topic sentence from your draft into a single paragraph. If your paragraph is well organized, coherent, and reflective of the substance of your essay, you have written well. If, on the other hand, your paragraph seems disordered, vague, or untidy, it is time to expand, condense, fine-tune, and consider your revision options.

This technique also works well for reviewing paragraph organization. Write each sentence on a separate note card, and then arrange the cards into a paragraph. You may discover issues that need attention, find that your initial arrangement is sufficient, or realize that an alternative organization communicates the essay's purpose more clearly.

## Share Your Draft

Having a friend or classmate read your essay is always a good idea. However, do not simply hand the essay to someone and expect constructive comments. Use an assessment sheet similar to the one shown in Figure 9.1, and ask your friend to fill it out as he or she reads your paper. This will help your peer give you constructive criticism rather than simply saying he or she likes your essay.

If your instructor asks you to participate in a revision workshop, be sure to take full advantage of the opportunity. Ask your peers to pay close attention to your work. Be prepared when you come to workshop day with the number of copies that you need, and also bring a variety of colored highlighters. Your instructor will probably give you an evaluation form to complete for a peer's paper; be a good reading partner, and fill it out completely and constructively. After you receive your essay copies back, ask questions of your peers or instructor if you do not understand a comment or correction. Your willingness to participate will be a model for others reading and reviewing your paper.

Whatever way you share your paper with others, be selective in the comments you choose to guide your revision. Be sure that the changes strengthen the paper's content, organization, and style. Also, keep in mind that writing is often a very personal experience, and some find it difficult to share their work. So, provide thoughtful, **constructive criticism** that will help your peers improve rather than discourage them.

## Titles

Most writers prefer to consider a title after they have completed and revised an entire draft. Now that your subject and focus, your tone, your audience and purpose are all clearly determined, you might try to capture the essence of this writing in a few words. After all, the title is the first thing your audience sees of your essay; why not establish an initial greeting that captures your whole discussion? Be accurate and specific in your title, providing more than the mere subject of your essay. The title should let the reader see the link between what it promises and what the essay delivers. You might include a key word from the focus of your discussion, but don't use a sentence as your title because the title should be concise and to the point. Be consistent with the tone; a serious essay is undermined by a flippant title. Use your imagination and be creative; strive to get the attention of your audience.

# Focus Secondarily on Editing

## Punctuation

- Do sentences have the correct closing punctuation?
- Are commas, semicolons, dashes, apostrophes, and other internal punctuation marks used correctly?
- Are quotations correctly introduced, punctuated, and carefully cited? Are quotation marks turned the right way, toward the quoted material?
- Are in-text citations correctly punctuated?

## Spelling

- Are all words spelled correctly? Remember that spell-checkers are not always foolproof! Check for commonly confused words.
- Have you used the correct forms? Double-check any abbreviations, contractions, or possessive nouns.
- Have you used hyphens correctly? Double-check any hyphenated adjectives.

## Capitalization and Italics

- Are words and quotations capitalized correctly?
- Are proper names and titles distinguished with appropriate capitalization and punctuation?

# Strategies for Editing

> "The time to begin writing an article is when you have finished it to your satisfaction. By that time you begin to clearly and logically perceive what it is you really want to say."
>
> —Mark Twain

Since editing comes towards the end of the writing process, it might be tempting to hurry through this step or skip it completely. Unfortunately, doing so can seriously undermine the quality of your writing. To many readers, editing errors seem careless or unprofessional. An essay dotted with spelling and punctuation errors suggests the author does not care enough about his or her ideas to ensure they are presented clearly and correctly.

Careful editing becomes especially important in high stakes situations. For example, if a scholarship or job search has been narrowed down to two equally qualified candidates, a carefully-edited essay or resume may give you an advantage. The scholarship committee may respect your attention to detail, or the hiring manager may select you because he or she knows that sending documents back for editing costs the company extra time. You can ensure your writing is not undermined by simple, avoidable mistakes by utilizing the following strategies for thoroughly editing your work.

## Set the Work Aside After Revising

Invest in a calendar that is only used for your writing class. Each time you receive an assignment, start with the due date and work your way back in the calendar, marking personal deadlines for a rough draft, revised draft, and edited draft. This will help you save enough time at the end of the writing process for editing and proofreading. Then, after you complete a revised draft, put your essay aside for a while. This will allow you to have some distance from the writing when you pick up the essay again to look for errors in mechanics or spelling.

## Keep Track of Your Editing Problem Areas

As you gain experience editing your work, you may notice reoccurring editing issues. To avoid repeating the same mistakes through the semester, use a chart such as the essay grid shown in Figure 9.1 to note the two or three most common problems your instructor or peers marked. Then, use the grid to check each essay before you turn it in. Tracking your problem areas will also help clarify the editing issues you should ask for addition help with during your next peer editing session or visit UCM's writing center. As you progress through the semester, note if you have been successful in eliminating these problem areas, and add other problem areas that pop up in later essays.

## Use Available Tools

When you edit, be sure to have a dictionary, thesaurus, and grammar handbook available. Do not postpone looking something up, and if you cannot find assistance by yourself, be sure to take advantage of on-campus editing resources.

## Use On-Campus Editing Resources

Even successful, published authors use editors to help polish their work. After all, a second pair of eyes can often spot errors that the author overlooked. As the author, you have read your essay multiple times and may see what you expect to see rather than what is actually printed on the page. While professional writers may hire a professional editor, your editor may be a classmate, a friend with a sharp eye for comma placement, or a tutor at the University of Central Missouri Learning Commons (https://www.ucmo.edu/learningcommons/)or Writing Center (www.ucmo.edu/ae/writing/). You might even visit your instructor during his or her office hours. Keep in mind that the key to successful editing is not necessarily memorizing every rule of grammar and mechanics. You can successfully edit and proofread your paper by using the numerous resources available on campus or online.

**Figure 9.1: Essay Grid**

| Essay | Area #1 | Area #2 | Area #3 | Area #4 | Area #5 | Area #6 |
|:-----:|:-------:|:-------:|:-------:|:-------:|:-------:|:-------:|
| 1 | | | | | | |
| 2 | | | | | | |
| 3 | | | | | | |
| 4 | | | | | | |
| 5 | | | | | | |

**Assignment 9.1**

**Create an Editor's Response**

On a graded essay, find at least two comments regarding mechanical issues, such as punctuation and grammar. Correct these on a separate sheet of paper. For each mechanical issue you correct:

- Quote the sentence where the error appears
- Explain what the issue is
- Explain in your own words why it was marked as an error
- Describe what you need to do to fix the error
- Fix the error, and rewrite the sentence demonstrating the correction

# Strategies for Proofreading

Be sure to take the time to proofread your essay carefully before turning it in; proofreading is the final step of the writing process. Use this step to focus on punctuation, spelling, capitalization, italics, and formatting. While computers have made it much easier to produce a professional-looking document, proofreading is still essential. Once again, you can break your essay into smaller levels by focusing in on one particular proofreading task at a time.

## Formatting

Once you have finalized the content of your essay, the final step in proofreading involves double checking the appearance of your writing. In academic writing, the layout and appearance of a written text is commonly referred to as the format. Refer to Appendices I and II for UCM's English Department guidelines for MLA formatting.

Check the following:

- Have you followed all of your instructor's directions about formatting?

- Are the margins correct?

- Is the spacing correct between words, sentences, and paragraphs?

- Is the heading (with information about you, your class, and your instructor) present and correct? Does it contain all of the required information in the correct order and format?

- Is there a title that is centered and spaced correctly, and not underlined, italicized, bolded, in quotation marks, or in a different font?

- Is there a header with your name and the page number in the upper, right corner of each page?

- If necessary, is there a Works Cited page that follows the required documentation style? (See Assignment 12.3.)

Individual classes, instructors, and assignments may call for slightly different formats; it is essential to check with both your instructor and your assignment sheet to ensure you have formatted the assignment correctly. Doing so shows that you care about the presentation of all your hard work.

Your teacher will likely use the following symbols for editing and proofreading; it is important that you are familiar with them.

**Table 9.1: Editing and Proofreading Symbols**

| | |
|---|---|
| agr | Agreement Problem |
| ⱱ̓ | Apostrophe |
| APA | APA Documentation |
| awk | Awkward Wording |
| [ ] | Brackets |
| cap | Capitalization |
| : | Colon |
| ⋀, | Comma |
| cs | Comma Splice |
| coor | Coordination |
| — | Dash |
| ℓ | Delete |
| ᵛⱯⱱ | Double Quotation Marks |
| . . . | Ellipsis Points |
| ! | Exclamation Point |
| frag | Fragment |
| fs | Fused Sentence |
| ⋀ | Insert |
| ital | Italics |
| lc | Lowercase |

| MLA | MLA Documentation |
|---|---|
| ¶ | Paragraph |
| / / | Parallelism |
| ( ) | Parentheses |
| ⊙ | Period |
| P/A | Pronoun/Antecedent Agreement |
| pro | Pronoun |
| ? | Question Mark |
| ⌃; | Semicolon |
| / | Slash |
| # | Space Needed |
| sp | Spelling |
| sub | Subordination |
| S/V | Subject/Verb Agreement |
| trans | Transition |
| ∼ | Transpose Two Elements |
| ⌐⸴ | Unnecessary Comma |
| wc | Word Choice |

# Part III:
# Writing for the World

# Chapter 10

# Introduction to Rhetoric

Rhetoric, or persuasive communication, happens all around us every day: in conversation at the grocery store, on blogs, on television, and in the classroom. In contemporary society, we constantly air our opinions about almost everything. Sometimes it is to convince others to share our opinions; sometimes the reason is to engage in a dialogue that will help us understand the world around us; sometimes it is to persuade others to action.

Argument is essential to human interaction and to society; it is through the interplay of ideas in argument that we discover answers to problems, try out new ideas, shape scientific experiments, communicate with family members, recruit others to join a team, and work out a variety of human interactions essential for society to function. When issues are complex, arguments do not result in the immediate persuasion of an audience; rather, argument is part of an ongoing conversation between concerned parties who seek resolution, rather than speedy answers.

As we discussed in Chapter 1, decorum is a familiar term we use today, mainly in reference to the observation of proper rules of behavior and speech. However, in ancient times, the term's meaning was much richer and more complex. Marcus Tullius Cicero, a Roman rhetorician and the first lawyer, used the term to describe the proper style and language to use in a given context. To observe the appropriate decorum, a speaker had to consider the audience and their social and economic backgrounds, the location in which the speech took place, what was happening in the world of politics, and many additional factors. If the speaker didn't follow decorum, miscommunication could easily occur, and while that was unhelpful to the speaker, it was particularly unhelpful to the members of the audience who needed to hear the speaker's message. So, decorum helped connect people who held different opinions. It helped them find some common ground so they could resolve their differences.

Cicero saw decorum as essential, not only to speeches, but to all aspects of life; he also acknowledged that it was difficult to achieve because of its complexity. Each speaking situation was different, and though certain stylistic features may work wonderfully in one setting, they may fail to work in a different setting. So, the ability to determine the proper decorum is tied to the ability to **analyze** and **evaluate** a situation as well.

# Rhetoric and Decorum

The first step to understanding decorum is to develop an understanding of rhetoric. **Rhetoric** is the art of persuasion. Many people think of rhetoric as the use of flowery speech used to mislead the public; phrases like "empty rhetoric" are often used in the media to describe political speeches. Such phrases suggest that rhetoric is meaningless, mere manipulation with no substance.

Rhetoricians see rhetoric as neutral; to them, it is an art that can be used both to manipulate for self-gain and to persuade people for ethical reasons, depending upon the intent of the speaker. Through the use of rhetoric, a speaker (or writer) sways an audience. In its most basic form, the study of rhetoric is the study of the persuasive power of language. As our culture has developed, rhetoric has evolved, and how we persuade has changed.

## The Importance of Understanding Rhetoric

Rhetoric provides a useful framework for looking at the world, and is a tool for evaluating and initiating communications. In the modern world, writing, communicating, and understanding persuasion are necessary skills. In the business world, those who can present effective arguments in writing are often the ones who are promoted. In addition, those who are able to evaluate the arguments presented to them, whether by politicians, advertisers, or even family members, are less likely to be swayed by logical fallacies or ill-supported research.

Also, writing rhetorically is a tool with sometimes surprising uses. Rhetoric helps writers reflect critically, which encourages deeper learning. Research shows that you are more likely to remember material you have written about rather than simply memorized. Also, through the process of writing, you may find new ideas and connections between topics that you might not otherwise have found. Thus, writing may lead to new discoveries.

# The Rhetorical Situation

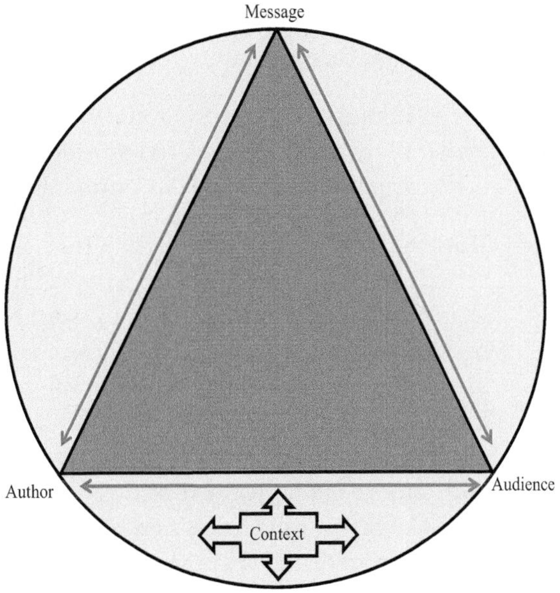

Rhetoric is persuasion through language. In order for persuasion to take place, an author must have a detailed understanding of his or her audience. Also, an author must have a message to impart to that audience. Finally, all of this takes place within a context (historical, social, etc.) All of these components make up the rhetorical situation. If illustrated visually, the rhetorical situation may look like Figure 10.1.

**Figure 10.1  The Rhetorical Situation**

Message

Author

Context

Audience

## Author

An author is anyone who wants to send a message through any means of communication. The author's **purpose** could be to persuade, or it could be something different. Some authors only want their audiences to hear their messages. Others want the audiences to learn something or to change their minds. Still others want the audiences to take action.

## Message

The message is the information the author wants to convey to the audience. A message can range from simple to complex. Simple messages are often imparted by advertisers (buy this book). More complex messages can come from a number of sources.

For example, an author can write a book encouraging people to look at an important issue differently. Although authors can send messages in a number of ways, written messages can be one of the most powerful, because language is subtle and complex. Nuances and connotations of words can add shades of meaning to a text, which causes the members of the audience to receive a variety of messages in different ways.

## Audience

One of the most important parts of the rhetorical situation is the audience. The audience can be any size—from one person to thousands of people. The audience is the person, or people, to whom the author wants to speak.

For example, when a presidential election takes place, each candidate has an audience. In simple terms, the presidential candidate's **primary audience** is the registered voters of the United States.

However, it is more complex than that. Each candidate knows that he has certain segments of the public who will not agree with him. For example, a Democratic candidate who is in favor of reducing the military budget will find little support among Republicans, especially those from military families. However, a Democratic candidate may be able to find support among moderates and independents. So he may choose to ignore states that have a strong Republican base, and he may spend more time speaking to states with a more moderate or mixed voting base. Even though the candidate wants to target moderates and independents, he will need to be very careful not to say anything that completely offends or alienates Republicans. In addition, he will have to be careful to make sure that Democrats don't feel neglected. If they do, he could easily lose the election. In this way, we can see that the political candidate must carefully tailor his message to each audience in order to have the desired, persuasive impact.

Every author faces a similar situation when he or she sends out a persuasive message. The author has a broad audience, which includes anyone who could potentially hear the message. But there is also a primary audience, a group of people who can be swayed, who are more likely to be convinced to agree with the author. The trick is to sway the target audience while retaining the necessary decorum to keep the **secondary audience** interested in the message.

An author must carefully consider what the audience wants in order to achieve decorum. The goal of the author is to win over the audience. The author does this by showing the audience why changing their views is a good idea—how they will benefit from their change of heart.

For example, in television ads that encourage people to give to charities for needy children, the focus is only partly on the starving children. The focus is also on how good it will make people feel if they do something to help a child. So, the ads focus on the audience, showing the audience what they get out of giving. That is how rhetoric works. The concerns of the audience have to be considered in order for rhetoric to be persuasive.

Often, the audience is influenced by a number of outside factors, and will only be receptive to an author's message under certain circumstances. It is then that *Kairos* comes into play. *Kairos* means "Fitting for the occasion," and it indicates the time that an audience is not only ready and receptive, but eager for the message that the author has to deliver. *Kairos* refers to the timeliness of a discussion.

## Context

The context is the situation within which the author's message occurs. For example, some messages only make sense when the historical situation is examined closely. If we were to read a rhetorical piece from the 18th century, we would have to understand something about what was going on at the time—we would have to study the history. Otherwise, elements of the text wouldn't make sense or we could mistakenly think the opposite of what the author intended. Sometimes, in order to understand how a situation is now, a person has to understand the history of how it evolved over time. However, even contemporary messages need to be placed within an historical context. Understanding the social context is also important. The **social context** is the determination of where the audience fits in society—this includes education level, income level, gender, race, and age of the members of the audience. The kind of language an author uses, the tone, and the style all differ depending on the social context. The messages that authors send to academic audiences, for example, are far different than the ones sent to the general public. Also, different academic disciplines have different terms and styles that they commonly use.

## Rhetorical Appeals

Knowing that appealing to the audience was important, classical rhetorician Aristotle argued that there are three types of appeals that are necessary for successful persuasive or argumentative communication. These three types of appeals are ethos, logos, and pathos.

## Ethos

**Ethos** demonstrates the authority and credibility of the speaker or writer. There are many ways to show an audience that the writer is credible, and as such should be listened to. Is this writer a well-known figure or expert in the subject of the argument? Does the writer have well-reasoned and legitimate information that proves to the audience that the writer is knowledgeable about the issues? Does this person have other credentials or characteristics that may demonstrate to the audience that she or he is dependable in this context, such as being a religious or political figure? The rhetorical situation, specifically the audience, will guide which characteristics can establish a writer's ethos.

## Logos

Appeals classified as **logos** are those that focus on logic, either by argumentative structure or evidence for the writer's claims. Modern logos, particularly used in researched argumentative writing, focuses on the use of credible evidence to support a thesis. This evidence may include texts, graphics, interviews, other qualitative data, or quantitative data. In many fields, the logos necessary to convince a particular audience will change based on the genre of the writing and the type of audience. Logos substantiates a writer's argument, and it also supports ethos by enhancing the writer's credibility.

## Pathos

**Pathos** is an appeal made to an audience's emotions. The types of emotions the writer should appeal to for a successful argument will depend on the rhetorical situation. A writer will often want to demonstrate a similarity to the audience, either as people sharing a common bond or sharing the same view of the subject at hand. This can include appealing to an audience's shared dreams or dilemmas. Sometimes the author may choose to appeal to an audience's fears; while this is negative on the surface, it can be necessary to sway an audience to agree with the speaker (such as with some literature in public health that encourages readers to make a lifestyle change in order to save their lives). Narrative techniques, such as use of metaphor and simile, and emotional diction are some ways to enhance pathos.

## Assignment 10.1

### Analyze an Audience

Select a group that you do not belong to and analyze it as a potential audience. Do this by locating a blog on the Internet that advocates a point of view different from your own. For example, if you believe in global warming, read a blog frequented by those who do not share that belief. If you are a Democrat, look for a Tea Party or Republican blog. Find a yoga blog if you are a football fan.

Read blog entries for a week and write a one-page analysis. Answer these questions:

1. What are the two or three issues of primary interest to the group? What is the general position on each issue?

2. Identify the audience. What kinds of people visit this blog? Where do they live? What is their educational level?

3. What is the extent of their knowledge about the issues of primary interest? Are they familiar with the evidence, or do they just repeat opinions?

4. What types of appeals would make a difference to the readers of this blog: ethos, pathos, or logos? How so?

# Chapter 11

# Visual Rhetoric

## Visual Rhetoric and Power

Aristotle defined rhetoric as "the faculty of discovering, in a given instance, the available means of persuasion," which we might paraphrase as the power to see the means of persuasion available in any given situation. Each part of this definition is important. Rhetoric is power; the person who is able to speak eloquently, and choose the most suitable arguments about a topic for a specific audience in a particular situation, is the person most likely to persuade. To Greeks and Romans, a person who could use rhetoric effectively was a person of influence and power because he could persuade his audience to action. The effective speaker could win court cases; the effective speaker could influence the passage or failure of laws; the effective speaker could send a nation to war or negotiate peace.

Rhetorical skills have conveyed power throughout the ages, though in our contemporary world, rhetoric is often displayed in written texts such as books, newspaper or magazine articles, or scientific reports, in addition to items such as speeches. Persuasive communication also can be expressed visually. For example, an illustration that accompanies a text or a cartoon conveys its own message. Indeed, in our highly visual society, with television, movies, video games, and the internet, images can sometimes persuade more powerfully than words alone.

**Visual rhetoric** is a part of our everyday lives; it is made up of images and text (or captioning) to convey a message to a particular audience. When we're in a conversation with someone, we use rhetoric on a conscious or subconscious level. If you go to class wearing the T-shirt of your favorite musician or band, you're ultimately sending a rhetorical message identifying yourself as a fan of that artist or group. When you go to a job interview, you usually wear your best clothing in order to persuade the interviewer that you are the best candidate. Subtle choices we make can have profound meanings.

If you've ever written a profile on a dating site, you've used rhetorical principles to convince an audience of potential partners to contact you or to write you back. You build ethos by highlighting the positive aspects of yourself or your educational background in order to build credibility among potential partners, and you establish pathos when you talk about an interest that is shared by a potential mate. When you pick a profile picture, you are making a visual argument about yourself to potential partners. Likewise, when you send silly Snapchats to your sister or best friend, but brush your hair and smile when you're chatting with a crush, you're making rhetorical choices.

Being able to use the tools of rhetoric effectively gives you the power to control your communication—both incoming and outgoing—and to impact your environment in a positive way.

## Encountering Visual Rhetoric

Why is a visual so powerful? Colors, shapes, and symbols impact viewers in ways text alone cannot. Many images present arguments, and, because they are visual, they communicate more quickly.

The images on the next page are covers from *GQ* magazine. On the left, Sacha Baron Cohen, as his character Bruno, graces the humor edition of the magazine in a pose echoing that of Jennifer Aniston, on the right, which was printed on a cover a few months previously. What do you think when you see a man positioned in a way that is typical for a scantily dressed (or nude) female? Is it funny? Why do you think so? Many think the image is simply an attempt at humor, but not everyone agrees about its message.

A photo's ability to persuade can be significant, whether it is a news photo or an advertisement. However, not everyone interprets images the same way, especially when they evoke stereotypes of gender, race, religion, or other sensitive issues. A posting on a blog called *thesocietypages.org* says of Cohen: "The contrast between the meaning of the pose (sexy and feminine) with the fact that he's male draws attention to how powerfully gendered the pose is... women look sexy when they pose like this, men look stupid when they do" (Wade). The blog is clearly stating that, behind the seemingly innocuous image, there is a clear connection to gender inequality.

## Responding to Visual Rhetoric

Methods of analyzing visual rhetoric draw upon several theoretical traditions. In art criticism, viewers may look for symbolism in an image or consider what meaning the artist was trying to convey. **Semiotics** views images as having **intertextuality**, as similar images come to have similar meanings, and those meanings may create similar emotions in the viewer. All of these elements are combined when an image is viewed rhetorically.

Rhetoricians, as you might expect, consider the argument that an image may present to a viewer. They think about how the subject of the image is presented in relation to other elements in the visual, how the image is cropped, and what types of lighting and colors are present. Rhetoricians also pay particular attention to the interplay between the visual image and any text that may appear with the image, and they also investigate how the combined elements may be used to construct an argument.

Courtesy BMW premium advertising.

In the BMW advertisement shown above, for example, a beautiful blonde-haired young woman is presented, presumably, without clothes, lying down with her hair artfully arranged in waves. *Salon* magazine reprinted a copy of the BMW advertisement pointing out that, "in small print scrawled across her bare shoulder, it reads: 'You know you're not the first.' As your eyes drift to the bottom of the advertisement—and the top of her chest—you learn that it's an advertisement for BMW's premium selection of used cars."

BMW is clearly using sexual appeal to attract viewers, and, of course, sexual appeal has been used for decades to sell a whole range of products. However, what do you think is BMW's argument? *Salon* thinks the ad is implying, "Used cars, used women," and that the ad gives a "whole new meaning" to BMW's slogan, printed in the ad: "Sheer Driving Pleasure." Do you agree with that analysis? Why or why not?

The image that appears below, surprisingly, isn't advertising a car. No, it is selling a community college, West Hills College; capitalizing on the idea that with all the money you would save by going to a community college, you could buy a nice car.

Courtesy West Hills College

Two years at West Hills College: $600
vs.
Two years at a UC school: $28,000*
**Why not spend $27,400 on something else?**

ONCE YOU GO HERE,
YOU CAN GO ANYWHERE.

WEST HILLS
COMMUNITY
COLLEGE
DISTRICT

1-800-266-1114 or www.westhillscollege.com

By investigating images carefully and looking more deeply, we can often see subtle ways in which we are being persuaded. By analyzing different aspects of images, we can break down the larger pieces of an image to look at small choices that impact viewers in large ways.

---

## Assignment 11.1
### Write a Caption for a Photo or a Pair of Photos

Choose a news photo or advertisement from a newspaper, magazine, or the Internet that presents an argument. Alternatively, compare two news photos or advertisements. Copy or paste the photo(s) onto a piece of paper, and then write a caption that expresses the argument(s) you see in the photo.

### Assignment 11.2

#### Interpret Advertisements

1. What is the symbolism of the beautiful young woman posed as she is in the BMW advertisement?

2. What do you think the tag line, "You know you're not the first," adds to the image? When you realize that the image is an ad for BMW used cars, does your interpretation of this tag line's meaning change?

3. Do you find the BMW advertisement amusing, objectionable, or appealing? Does it make you want to buy a used BMW?

4. What are the creators of the West Hills College advertisement trying to say by showing the image of the student sitting on the car?

5. The use of fonts is another important element in transmitting a message in an advertisement. In the West Hills College ad, why are the words "and save" written in a different font and inserted with the caret?

6. As a college student, would you be convinced by the West Hills advertisement? Why or why not? What elements exist in the ad that would or would not convince you to attend the college mentioned?

### Assignment 11.3

#### Find Advertisements with Effective Arguments

Bring an advertisement to class that you think makes an effective argument. It can be torn from a magazine or downloaded from the internet. In a small group, evaluate each advertisement for its effectiveness in selling something, and choose the one with the most effective argument. Present your choice to the class along with an explanation of what elements make it effective.

# Working with Sources

# Chapter 12

As a student, you are expected to join academic conversations already in progress. How do you do that? How do you know what kind of response is appropriate?

## Becoming Part of the Academic Conversation

Have you ever entered a party where everyone is talking excitedly? Most likely, you paused near the doorway to get a sense of who was there and what they were discussing before you decided who to talk to and what to say. Or, have you taken part in a Facebook group or listserv discussion group? If so, you know it is a good idea to "lurk" for a while before asking questions or contributing a remark.

Writing an academic paper involves a similar process. You read about a subject until you have a good grasp of the points authorities are debating. Then you find a way to integrate your own ideas about that subject with the ideas of others and create an informed contribution to the conversation.

The following introductions to movie reviews demonstrate that the writers understand the films and have interesting things to say about them; they also display knowledge of what others have written about the films, whether the writers agree with those evaluations or not.

- Roger Ebert claims that audience members who haven't seen the first two *Lord of the Rings* films (Peter Jackson, 2001, 2002) will likely "be adrift during the early passages of [the third] film's 200 minutes." But then again, Ebert continues, "to be adrift occasionally during this nine-hour saga comes with the territory" (par. 3). Ebert, though, misses one crucial fact regarding *Lord of the Rings: The Return of the King* (2003). This third installment opens with a flashback intended to familiarize new spectators about what happened in the previous two films. Within these five minutes, the audience discovers how Gollum (Andy Serkis) came to be corrupt through the destructive power of the Ring. The viewer, therefore, will not necessarily be "adrift," as Ebert claims, since the lighting, setting, and sound in the opening of *The Return of the King* show the lighter, more peaceful world before Gollum finds the ring, compared to the darker, more sinister world thereafter.

- "It's hard to resist a satire, even when it wobbles, that insists the most unbelievable parts are the most true" (*Rolling Stone* par. 1). This is Peter Travers's overarching view of Grant Heslov's satire, *The Men Who Stare at Goats* (2009). Travers is correct here; after all, *Goats*'s opening title card, which reads, "More of this is real than you would believe," humorously teases the viewer that some of the film's most "unbelievable parts" will, in fact, offer the most truth. We experience this via Bill Wilson's (Ewan McGregor) interview of an ex "psy-ops" soldier, when Wilson's life spirals out of control, and all the other farfetched actions presenting "reality." But again, it is the film's opening—specifically, its setting, camera movements and angles, dialogue, effects, and ambient noise—that sets the foundation for an unbelievably realistic satire.

In both of these introductions, the students quote reviews by professional film critics and respond to the critics' opinions. Moreover, the students continue their arguments by using the critics' ideas as springboards for their own arguments. These students have learned how to counter positions advocated by authorities without losing their own voices. If the rest of their essays continue as they have begun, the students will have written essays to which others can reply, thus continuing the conversation.

## Using Common Knowledge and Personal Experience to Join the Conversation

Most people know that George Washington was the first president of the United States. Most people have heard Martin Luther King Jr.'s famous proclamation, "I Have a Dream." These types of facts and phrases are considered **common knowledge** and do not need to be cited. If you are well-read or knowledgeable on a certain topic, it may be difficult to distinguish between common knowledge and information you have gathered in your studies. A good rule of thumb is to imagine asking ten random people about the information. If most of them would know the answer, then the information is common knowledge. If not, you should search out a source and cite the information.

Similarly, lived experience need not be cited. If you grew up in a small Midwestern town and witnessed first-hand the way businesses closed and people moved away when the new highway diverted traffic, you don't need to find a source. You can use your **personal experience** as evidence. However, you could also combine your description of rural decline with some cited statistics to back up your point and enhance your credibility.

## Reading to Write, Reading to Cite

However, in many writing situations, you will be asked to include secondary source material to support your argument, help prove your claims, or situate your ideas within the academic conversation. These **secondary sources** take many forms: statistics, compelling quotes from a popular author, examples, lines from a speech, passages from historical documents, song lyrics, or ideas summarized from a well-researched book.

As you read secondary sources, take note of interesting ideas and phrases that you might use later in your writing. You can either copy the information into a notebook or onto an index card. Be certain to include the author's name, the page number, the title, and the location of the information so you can find it again later. Carefully documenting your sources as you read will save you time when you add citations to your final draft. It can also prevent unintentional plagiarism since it's easy to read something and then forget where you first encountered the information.

## Using Secondary Sources to Join the Conversation

Any time you include the words or ideas of another writer in your writing, you must **document** that information appropriately. To **cite** information is to acknowledge the original source of the information.

### Ways to Use Sources in Your Essay

Once you have found a piece of information you plan to include in your essay, the next step is to decide how to include it. There are three ways to incorporate secondary sources into your writing.

### Quotation

A direct **quotation** uses the author's exact words as they appeared in the original source. The words are placed in quotation marks. Quotations lend themselves to short passages where the author's word choices or turn-of-phrase are as important as the idea itself.

Sherman Alexie observes, "A smart Indian is a dangerous person, widely feared and ridiculed by Indians and non-Indians alike" (140).

## Summary

When you **summarize**, you put the author's main ideas in your own words. Summaries are useful because they allow you to provide a short overview of the author's message. You may summarize an entire article into a few sentences. As you translate the author's ideas into your writing, be careful that you do not change or distort the author's meaning. Before you summarize, read through the passage multiple times to insure you are not misrepresenting the author or taking his or her ideas out of context.

> In Sherman Alexie's short story "Superman and Me," he discusses the negative stereotypes of Indian children. He explains how he used reading to overcome these stereotypes and challenges (139-41).

## Paraphrase

While summaries provide a short, general overview of the author's ideas, a **paraphrase** focuses on a single point. Like a summary, you rewrite a paraphrase in your own words. However, paraphrases tend to be longer and more detailed than summaries. Paraphrasing is a useful strategy when the author makes a useful point, but there is no specific need to use the author's exact words.

> Alexie claims that books and reading saved his life by allowing him to escape the confines of negative stereotypes. He used these experiences to become a successful writer and pass his knowledge to future generations (141).

If you compare the summary and paraphrase, you will notice that while they are a similar length, the summary focuses on a wider range of topics. The summary briefly covers a large section of the essay, while the paraphrase goes into more detail about a single paragraph.

## Adding words to a quotation

Use square brackets [ ] to point out words or phrases that are not part of the original text.

→ She said, "When we entered the People's Republic of China, [Dunkirk and I] noticed that the signage began dropping English translations" (Donelson 141).

You can also add your own comments inside a quotation by using square brackets. For example, you can add the word *sic* to a quotation when you know that there is an error.

➔ She said, "When we entered the People's Repulic [sic] of China, we noticed that the signage began dropping English translations" (Donelson 141).

## Omitting words in a quotation

Use an ellipsis ( . . . ) to represent words that you delete from a quotation. The ellipsis begins with a space, then has three periods with spaces between them, and then ends with a space.

➔ Frank Donelson, author of *Signs in Space,* remarks, "The Great Wall . . . can be seen from space. When we reach a time when advertisements can be seen from space, we have probably gone too far" (178).

If you omit words at the end of a quotation, and that is also the end of your sentence, use an ellipsis plus a period with no space before the ellipsis or after the period.

➔ Frank Donelson, author of *Signs in Space,* remarks, "The Great Wall is something that can be seen from space. When we reach a time when advertisements can be seen from space, we have probably gone too far. . ." (178).

The choice between quoting, summarizing, and paraphrasing depends on your purpose. Quotations allow an author to speak for him - or herself. As such, quotations are ideal for transcribing memorable phrases or carefully analyzing an author's language. When you quote an author, there's less risk of misrepresenting the author's ideas. However, quoting long, unmemorable passages can be perceived as lazy. Quotations can quickly overshadow your own writing as your essay becomes a patchwork of quotations rather than a unified piece of writing. Summary demonstrates your ability to condense an author's argument down to its essential points. With a summary, you can quickly cover the source material and move on to your message. Similarly, a paraphrase allows you to incorporate useful facts and information while still maintaining your distinctive voice and style.

## Assignment 12.1

### Write a Summary

**Part 1:** Put away everything but a piece of paper and a writing instrument. Take a few minutes and write down everything you remember from the reading. When you are finished, underline the points that you think are the most important. Do this from memory; don't use your notes or refer to the essays.

**Part 2:** On a separate sheet of paper, write a summary of the reading. You may now pull out your notes and copy of the original essay.

**Part 3:** When everyone is finished, exchange summaries with one of your classmates. Read your classmate's summary.

1. Check to see if your classmate's summary has any patch writing.

2. Also, check to see if your classmate included his or her personal opinion in the summary. Summaries should be free of personal opinions—they are restatements of what someone else thinks.

3. Finally, take out your first piece of paper, where you wrote down the main points from the essay. Did your classmate include the ideas that you thought were the most important in his or her summary? If not, let your classmate know.

   Make comments on your classmate's summary to let them know what they are doing well and where they could improve. Return your classmate's summary. Make sure to sign your name.

**Part 4:** Read the comments that your classmates put on your summary.

You may ask questions for clarification if you like. Next, using your notes and the original essay, revise your summary.

**Part 5:** Homework Assignment: At home, type up your summary. Revise it again as you type, making sure that you:

1. Do not use any patch writing.

2. Address the key points in the reading.

3. Do not include your personal opinion.

## Why You Must Cite Sources

When you cite sources in your essay, you demonstrate your understanding of the academic conversation. You show readers that you are aware of what other people are saying about the topic. Doing so helps establish your ethos, as a writer. Furthermore, you can use other authors to support the point you are making in your essay. Rather than asking readers to believe you because you "say so," you provide proof that knowledgeable individuals agree with you or that research supports your claim. However, your sources do not always have to agree with you. You can illustrate what others believe and then explain why you disagree. Presenting the other side of a debate actually strengthens your writing because it shows that you are aware of the complexity of the topic.

Citing and documenting your sources is also important for avoiding plagiarism. Different universities and publications have different definitions of plagiarism. You can find the University of Central Missouri's Academic Honesty Policy in Appendix III in the back of this book. However, generally speaking, plagiarism is the unaccredited use of another person's words or ideas. Plagiarism can be both intentional and unintentional.

**Plagiarism includes:**

- Buying, stealing, or borrowing a paper

- Paying someone to write your paper

- Copying sections of text from a book or website without quotation marks or giving credit to the original author

- Combining sentences and paragraphs from other writers and including them in your paper without citations (**patch writing**)

Bottom line: include a citation any time you use words, ideas, or information that originated from someone else. Give credit where credit is due and acknowledge the writers who have informed and inspired your writing.

## How to Cite Sources

Depending on what type of essay you are writing or which type of course you are writing for, you will need to choose a documentation style and continue with that style for the entire essay. Two of the most common styles, especially for freshman and sophomore students, are MLA (Modern Language Association) and APA (American Psychological Association).

When you write in composition, language, linguistics, and literature courses, you will be asked to use documentation guidelines created by the Modern Language Association. *The MLA Handbook for Writers of Research Papers* provides a full description of the conventions used by this particular community of writers; updates to the *MLA Handbook* can be found at www. mla.org.

MLA guidelines require that you give both an **in-text citation** and a **Works Cited page** entry for any and all sources you use. Using accurate in-text citations helps guide your reader to the appropriate entry on the Works Cited page.

This section provides a very brief overview of MLA documentation style and an explanation of the most commonly used MLA documentation formats.

## MLA In-text Citations

In-text citations (also called parenthetical citations) point readers to where they can find more information about your researched supporting materials. When you use MLA documentation style, you need to indicate the author's last name and the location of the source material (page or paragraph number). Where this in-text information is placed depends on how you want to phrase the sentence that is summarized, paraphrased, or quoted. Be sure that the in-text citation guides the reader clearly to the source in the Works Cited, where complete information about the source is given.

The following are some of the most common examples of parenthetical citations.

### Author's name in text

When using a parenthetical reference to a single source that is already named in the sentence, use this form: (Page number). Note that the period goes after the parentheses.

➔ Stephanie Jones, author of *The Signs of Trouble*, describes "excessive sleeping, refraining from eating, and lying about simple things" as signs to look for when parents are concerned about their children (63).

### Author's name in reference

When the author's name is not included in the preceding sentence, use this form for the parenthetical information at the end of the sentence: (Author's

Last Name Page number). Note that there is no comma between the name and page in an MLA parenthetical reference, and also note that the period comes at the end of the sentence after the parentheses.

➔ When a teenager sleeps more than 10 hours per night, it is time to question whether she is having significant problems (Jones 63).

## No author given

When a work has no credited author, use a clipped version of the work's title.

➔ In a recent *Time* article, a list of 30 common signs of teenage trouble cites lack of sleep as the most common sign ("Thirty" 3).

## Online sources

In the MLA documentation style, online or electronic sources have their own formatting guidelines since these types of sources rarely give specific page numbers.

The MLA recommends that you include in the text, rather than in an in-text citation, the name(s) of the person (e.g., author, editor, director, performer) that begins the matching Works Cited entry. For instance, the following is the recommended way to begin an in-text citation for an online source:

➔ Roger Ebert says that Shyamalan "plays the audience like a piano" in the film *Signs* (par. 8).

If the author or creator of the website uses paragraph or page numbers, use these numbers in the parenthetical citation. If no numbering is used, do not use or add numbers to the paragraphs, pages, or parenthetical citation.

When website does not number paragraphs ➔ In his review of the film *Signs*, Roger Ebert says that Shyamalan "does what Hitchcock said he wanted to do, and plays the audience like a piano."

When website numbers paragraphs ➔ In his review of the film *Signs*, Roger Ebert says that Shyamalan "does what Hitchcock said he wanted to do, and plays the audience like a piano" (par. 8).

## Assignment 12.2

### Write In-text Citations

Directions: Below are four example sources. Put the correct information in the parentheses for an MLA in-text citation.

**From page 89 of the book:**

Bazerman, Charles. *Shaping Written Knowledge: The Genre and*

*Activity of the Experimental Article in Science.* Madison, Wis.:

U of Wisconsin P, 1988. Print.

Yet, it could also be the case that "genre and activity are more closely related than we had previously thought" (          ).

**From page 340 of the article:**

Bodemer, Brett. "The Importance of Search as Intertextual Practice

for Undergraduate Research." *College and Research Libraries*

73.4 (2012): 336–348. Print.

Bodemer, however, suggests that "increasingly, the ability to search

well on the Internet will be as important a literacy skill as

reading or writing" (          ).

**From a magazine's web-only article:**

"Electronic Education: Flipping the Classroom." *The Economist* 17

Sept. 2011. *The Economist.* Web. 25 Apr. 2012.

*The Economist* has reported that "flipping the classroom is

the new teaching technique of the 21st century classroom"

(          ).

**From page 192 of the chapter:**

Schwartz, Daniel L. et al. "Toward the Development of Flexibly
Adaptive Instructional Designs." *Instructional Design Theories
and Models: Volume II.* Ed. C.M. Reigelut. Hillside, NJ: Erlbaum,
1999. 183–213. Print.

In a study performed by Schwartz et al., students found adaptive
classroom designs more engaging and, finally, more educational
(          ).

## MLA Works Cited Page

If you cite any sources within a paper, be sure to include a Works Cited at
the end of the paper. Here are some general formatting guidelines to follow
when setting up a Works Cited.

1. Put the Works Cited at the end of your paper as a separate page.
   You can insert a page break.

2. Use one-inch margins on all sides.

3. Include any header used on the Works Cited.

4. Center the title (Works Cited) at the top of the page with no
   underlining, quotation marks, or italics.

5. Place the first line of each entry flush with the left margin.
   Indent any additional lines of the entry one-half inch (or one
   tab). This is called hanging indent.

6. Double space the entries in the Works Cited; do not add any
   extra spaces between entries.

7. Alphabetize the Works Cited by the author's last name. If the
   cited source does not have an author, alphabetize by the first
   word of the title of the source. Use the first major word in each
   entry, not including articles such as a, an, or the, to determine
   the alphabetical order.

8. Put author's last name first (e.g., Ebert, Roger). Reverse only
   the first author's name. If more than one author, follow the first
   author's name with a comma, and add the other author names
   in the order of first then last names (e.g., Ebert, Roger, and
   Gene Siskel).

9. Capitalize all words in titles except for articles, conjunctions, and short prepositions. Always capitalize the first word of a title or subtitle.

10. Use quotation marks for titles of shorter works, including articles, book chapters, episodes on television or radio, poems, and short stories.

11. Italicize the titles of longer works, including albums or CDs, art pieces, books, films, journals, magazines, newspapers, and television shows.

12. Give the edition number for works with more than one edition (e.g., *MLA Handbook for Writers of Research Papers, 7th edition*).

13. Use the word *Print* after print sources and *Web* (followed by date of access) for Internet or Web sources.

The following are some of the most common types of sources Composition students might use.

## Print Sources

### Books (includes brochures, pamphlets, and graphic novels)

Author's Name. *Title of Book*. Place of publication: Publisher, date of publication. Print.

> ➔ Lansky, Doug. *Signspotting*. Oakland, CA: Lonely Planet, 2005. Print.

Use the state after the city only if the city is not one that would be commonly known or if there may be more than one commonly known city by that name.

### Books with two or more authors

A comma is used between the authors' names, even if there are only two authors.

First Author's Last name, First name, and second Author's full name. *Title of Book*. Place of publication: Publisher, date of publication. Print.

> ➔ Maasik, Sonia, and Jack Soloman. *Signs of Life in the USA: Readings on Popular Culture for Writers*. 6th edition. Boston: Bedford/St. Martin's, 2008. Print.

## Two books by the same author

Use three hyphens and a period in place of the author name(s) in the consecutive entries. Be sure the entries are in alphabetical order.

→Maasik, Sonia, and Jack Soloman. *California Dreams and Realities: Readings for Critical Thinkers and Writers.* 3rd edition. Boston: Bedford/St. Martin's, 2004. Print.

→---. *Signs of Life in the USA: Readings on Popular Culture for Writers.* 6th edition. Boston: Bedford/St. Martin's, 2008. Print.

## Work within an anthology

Author's Name. "Title of Work." *Title of Anthology.* Ed. Editor's Name(s). Place of publication: Publisher, date. Pages. Print.

→Tan, Amy. "Mother Tongue." *The Norton Field Guide to Writing.* Ed. Richard Bullock, et al.  New York: Norton, 2010. 564-70. Print.

## Article in a scholarly journal

Author's Name. "Title of the Article." *Journal Title* vol. number (date of publication): pages. Print.

→Holbrook, Teri. "An Ability Traitor at Work: A Treasonous Call to Subvert Writing from Within." *Qualitative Inquiry* 16.3 (2010): 171-83. Print.

## Article in a newspaper

Note: when citing English language newspapers, use the name on the masthead but be sure to omit any introductory article (*New York Times*, not *The New York Times*).

Author's Name. "Title of Article." *Newspaper Title* Day Month Year: pages. Print.

→Genzlinger, Neil. "Autism is Another Thing that Families Share." *New York Times* 6 Apr. 2010: A4. Print.

## Article in a magazine

Note:  Include the day only if the magazine is published on a weekly or bi-weekly basis.

Author's Name. "Title of Article." *Magazine Title* Day Month Year: pages. Print.

→Musico, Christopher. "Sign 'Em Up!" *CRM Magazine* Nov. 2009: 49. Print.

## Review

Reviewer's Name. "Title of Review." Rev. of *Title of Work*, by name of author (editor, director, etc.). *Journal or Newspaper Title* Day Month Year: pages. Print.

→Ebert, Roger. "A Monosyllabic Superhero Who Wouldn't Pass the Turing Test." Rev. of *X-Men Origins: Wolverine*, by Dir. Gavin Hood. *Chicago Sun-Times* 29 Apr. 2009: E4. Print.

## Online Sources

## Website

Author's Name (if author given). *Name of Page*. Name of institution or organization associated with the website, Date of posting/revision. Web. Date of access.

→*Services Locator*. United States Post Office, 2010. Web. 9 Feb. 2010.

## Article on a Website (including blogs and wikis)

Note: If there is no author given, begin the citation with the article title.

Author's Name. "Article Title." *Name of Website*. Name of institution or organization associated with the website, Date of posting/revision. Web. Date of access.

→"China's Traditional Dress: Qipao." *China Today*, Oct. 2001. Web. 9 Feb. 2010.

→Ebert, Roger. "Signs." *rogerebert.com Movie Reviews*. *Chicago Sun-Times*, 2 Aug. 2002. Web. 9 Feb. 2010.

## Online newspaper or magazine

Author's Name. "Title of Article." *Newspaper Title* Day Month Year: pages. Web. Date of access.

→Bailey, Holly. "The Sign of the Red Truck." *Newsweek* 2007: 1. Web. 9 Feb. 2010.

## Online journal article

Author's Name. "Title of Article." *Title of Journal* Vol. Issue (Year): pages.
  Web. Date of access.

➔ Austen, Veronica. "Writing Spaces: Performances of the Word."
  *Kairos* 8.1 (2003): n. pag. Web. 9 Feb. 2010.

## Other Commonly Used Sources

### Television or radio program

"Title of Episode or Segment." *Title of Program or Series*. Name of
  network. Call letters and city of the local station (if applicable).
  Broadcast date. Medium of reception (e.g., Radio, Television).
  Supplemental information (e.g., Transcript).

➔ "Signs and Wonders." *The X Files*. FOX. 23 Jan. 2000. Television.

### Sound recording

Artist/Band. "Song Title." *Title of Album*. Manufacturer, year of issue.
  Medium (e.g., Audiocassette, CD, Audiotape, LP, Digital download).

➔ Five Man Electrical Band. "Signs." *Good-byes and Butterflies*.
  Lionel Records, 1970. LP.

➔ Tesla. "Signs." *Five Man Acoustical Jam*. Geffen, 1990. CD.

### Film

*Title*. Dir. Director's Name. Perf. Actor's Name(s) (if relevant).
  Distributor, year of release. Medium.

➔ *Signs*. Dir. M. Night Shyamalan. Perf. Mel Gibson. Touchstone,
  2002. Film.

You may also include other information about the film, such as the names of
the writers, performers, and producers, after the director's name.

➔ *Signs*. Dir. M. Night Shyamalan. Perf. Mel Gibson. Ex. Prod.
  Kathleen Kennedy. Touchstone, 2002. Film.

If you would like to highlight the specific contribution of one actor, director,
or writer, you may begin the entry with that person's name, as you do with
an author for a book.

➜ Phoenix, Joaquin, perf. *Signs*. Dir. M. Night Shyamalan. Touchstone, 2002. Film.

## Advertisement

Note: print and television advertisements are formatted differently.

Name of product, company, or institution. Advertisement. Publisher date of publication. Medium of publication.

➜ SunChips. Advertisement. *Newsweek* 15 Jan. 2010: 33. Print.

➜ SunChips. Advertisement. NBC. 15 Jan. 2010. Television.

## Painting, sculpture, or photograph

Artist's Name. *Title*. Creation date (if known). Medium of Composition. Name of institution that houses the work or the individual who owns the work, City.

➜ da Vinci, Leonardo. *Mona Lisa*. c. 1503-6. Oil on Poplar. Louvre, Paris.

## Interview

Interviewee's Name. Descriptive Title of Interview (e.g., Personal, Telephone, Webcam). Date of interview.

➜ Elbow, Peter. Personal Interview. 1 Jan. 2009.

## Sample Works Cited Using MLA

Following is an example of how a completed Works Cited would look at the end of your paper. You can find further examples of Works Cited Pages after the student sample essays in the back of *Decorum*, as well as *Decorum's* list of cited sources on page 203.

---

Your Last name 14

Works Cited

Ebert, Roger. "Signs." *rogerebert.com* Movie Reviews. *Chicago Sun-*

*Times*. 2 Aug. 2002. Web. 9 Feb. 2010.

Five Man Electrical Band. "Signs." *Good-byes and Butterflies.* Lionel

Records, 1970. LP.

*Signs*. Dir. M. Night Shyamalan. Perf. Mel Gibson. Touchstone, 2002.

Film.

Stephens, Liberty. "The Signs of the Times." MLA Annual Convention.

Hilton Downtown, New York. 28 Dec. 2009. Address.

## Assignment 12.3
### Create a Works Cited Page

Directions: Insert all needed punctuation and formatting into the following MLA Works Cited entries. The type of source is listed after each.

Ackerman  John M  Reading  Writing  and Knowing: The Role of Disciplinary Knowledge in Comprehension and Composing Research in the Teaching of English 25.2  1991  133–178 Print  **(article in a journal)**

Baddeley  Alan  Working Memory  New York  Oxford University Press  1986  Print **(book)**

Barlow  John Perry  The Economy of Ideas  Wired Mar  1994  Web 17 June 2013 **(article in a magazine)**

Flower  Linda  and John R  Hayes   A Cognitive Process Theory of Writing  College Composition and Communication 32.4 1981  365–387  Print **(article in a journal)**

Hacker  Douglas J  Matt C  Keener  and John Kircher  Writing Is Applied Metacognition  Handbook of Metacognition in Education  1st ed  Ed  Douglas J  Hacker  John Dunlosky and Arthur C  Graesser  New York  Routledge  2009  Print **(chapter in a book or anthology)**

Rounsaville  Angela  Rachel Goldberg  and Anis Bawarshi  From Incomes to Outcomes: FYW Students' Knowledge  Meta-Cognition  and the Question of Transfer  WPA: Writing Program Administration 32.1 2008  97–112  Print **(article in a journal)**

# Part IV: Readings

## A Note on the Readings:

Each of the following essays covers a variety of topics; however, some essays discuss the same topic from a different angle or perspective. As you read, consider how these essays are similar and different. Ask yourself: what ideas, writing techniques, or rhetorical strategies connect these essays? Writing is a process that you learn by writing. However, humans are also wired to pick up language. Small children, for example, acquire most of their language by listening to the language spoken around them. While parents may actively speak or read to their children with the intention of teaching, most language development occurs as children are immersed in a world of words. Similarly, writers learn while they read the work of skilled writers. You can take an active role in the learning process by taking note of what the writers say and how they say it.

The questions that follow each reading may be read before the essay to guide your reading or afterward to review your understanding of the material. The questions are divided into three categories:

**Content** questions focus on *what* the author said. These questions will help you review the information presented in the essay. You can use these questions to gauge your reading comprehension.

Writing is a **craft** and writers continually make choices about how to effectively communicate with their audience. These questions focus on *how* the writer communicates their ideas. You can use these questions to study how writers use (or don't use) the writing techniques and rhetorical strategies introduced in *Decorum*.

The final questions are "big questions" for **contemplation**. They have no right or easy answers. Rather, these questions invite you to think more deeply on the *ideas* discussed in the essay. You can use these questions to engage further with the material, open up discussion, or inspire your own writing.

# Shitty First Drafts

## by Anne Lamott

*Anne Lamott has lived in the San Francisco area for most of her life. Her father, Kenneth Lamott, was a writer whose death from a brain tumor helped inspire her first novel,* Hard Laughter *(1980). Lamott has subsequently written several novels and works of non-fiction, typically from an autobiographical perspective. This reading is taken from 1994's* Bird by Bird: Some Instructions on Writing and Life; *in it she discusses the writing process and provides advice for those embarking on it.*

Now, practically even better news than that of short assignments is the idea of shitty first drafts. All good writers write them. This is how they end up with good second drafts and terrific third drafts. People tend to look at successful writers, writers who are getting their books published and maybe even doing well financially, and think that they sit down at their desks every morning feeling like a million dollars, feeling great about who they are and how much talent they have and what a great story they have to tell; that they take in a few deep breaths, push back their sleeves, roll their necks a few times to get all the cricks out, and dive in, typing fully formed passages as fast as a court reporter. But this is just the fantasy of the uninitiated. I know some very great writers, writers you love who write beautifully and have made a great deal of money, and not one of them sits down routinely feeling wildly enthusiastic and confident. Not one of them writes elegant first drafts. All right, one of them does, but we do not like her very much. We do not think that she has a rich inner life or that God likes her or can even stand her. (Although when I mentioned this to my priest friend Tom, he said you can safely assume you've created God in your own image when it turns out that God hates all the same people you do.)

Very few writers really know what they are doing until they've done it. Nor do they go about their business feeling dewy and thrilled. They do not type a few stiff warm-up sentences and then find themselves bounding along like huskies across the snow. One writer I know tells me that he sits down every morning and says to himself nicely, "It's not like you don't have a choice, because you do—you can either type or kill yourself." We all often feel like we are pulling teeth, even those writers whose prose ends up being the most natural and fluid. The right words and sentences just do not come pouring out like ticker tape most of the time. Now, Muriel Spark is said to have felt that she was taking dictation from God every morning—sitting there, one

Lamott, Anne. "Shitty First Drafts." *Bird by Bird: Some Instructions on Writing and Life.* New York: Pantheon Books, 1995. 21-27. Rpt. in *Decorum.* Ed. Kristina Gladfelter and Melody Niesen. Revised 2nd ed. Southlake, TX: Fountainhead, 2016. 125-128. Print.

supposes, plugged into a Dictaphone, typing away, humming. But this is a very hostile and aggressive position. One might hope for bad things to rain down on a person like this.

For me and most of the other writers I know, writing is not rapturous. In fact, the only way I can get anything written at all is to write really, really shitty first drafts. The first draft is the child's draft, where you let it all pour out and then let it romp all over the place, knowing that no one is going to see it and that you can shape it later. You just let this childlike part of you channel whatever voices and visions come through and onto the page. If one of the characters wants to say, "Well, so what, Mr. Poopy Pants?," you let her. No one is going to see it. If the kid wants to get into really sentimental, weepy, emotional territory, you let him. Just get it all down on paper, because there may be something great in those six crazy pages that you would never have gotten to by more rational, grown-up means. There may be something in the very last line of the very last paragraph on page six that you just love, that is so beautiful or wild that you now know what you're supposed to be writing about, more or less, or in what direction you might go—but there was no way to get to this without first getting through the first five and a half pages.

I used to write food reviews for *California* magazine before it folded. (My writing food reviews had nothing to do with the magazine folding, although every single review did cause a couple of canceled subscriptions. Some readers took umbrage at my comparing mounds of vegetable puree with various ex-presidents' brains.) These reviews always took two days to write. First I'd go to a restaurant several times with a few opinionated, articulate friends in tow. I'd sit there writing down everything anyone said that was at all interesting or funny. Then on the following Monday I'd sit down at my desk with my notes, and try to write the review. Even after I'd been doing this for years, panic would set in. I'd try to write a lead, but instead I'd write a couple of dreadful sentences, xx them out, try again, xx everything out, and then feel despair and worry settle on my chest like an x-ray apron. It's over, I'd think, calmly. I'm not going to be able to get the magic to work this time. I'm ruined. I'm through. I'm toast. Maybe, I'd think, I can get my old job back as a clerk-typist. But probably not. I'd get up and study my teeth in the mirror for a while. Then I'd stop, remember to breathe, make a few phone calls, hit the kitchen and chow down. Eventually I'd go back and sit down at my desk, and sigh for the next ten minutes.

Finally I would pick up my one-inch picture frame, stare into it as if for the answer, and every time the answer would come: all I had to do was to write a really shitty first draft of, say, the opening paragraph. And no one was going to see it. So I'd start writing without reining myself in. It was almost just typing, just making my fingers move. And the writing would be terrible. I'd write a lead paragraph that was a whole page, even though the entire review could only be three pages long, and then I'd start writing up descriptions of the food, one dish at a time, bird by bird, and the critics would be sitting on my shoulders, commenting like cartoon characters. They'd be pretending to snore, or rolling their eyes at my overwrought descriptions, no matter how hard I tried to tone those descriptions down, no matter how conscious I was of what a friend said to me gently in my early days of restaurant reviewing. "Annie," she said, "it is just a piece of *chicken*. It is just a bit of *cake*."

But because by then I had been writing for so long, I would eventually let myself trust the process—sort of, more or less. I'd write a first draft that was maybe twice as long as it should be, with a self-indulgent and boring beginning, stupefying descriptions of the meal, lots of quotes from my black-humored friends that made them sound more like the Manson girls than food lovers, and no ending to speak of. The whole thing would be so long and incoherent and hideous that for the rest of the day I'd obsess about getting creamed by a car before I could write a decent second draft. I'd worry that people would read what I'd written and believe that the accident had really been a suicide, that I had panicked because my talent was waning and my mind was shot.

The next day, though, I'd sit down, go through it all with a colored pen, take out everything I possibly could, find a new lead somewhere on the second page, figure out a kicky place to end it, and then write a second draft. It always turned out fine, sometimes even funny and weird and helpful. I'd go over it one more time and mail it in. Then, a month later, when it was time for another review, the whole process would start again, complete with the fears that people would find my first draft before I could rewrite it.

Almost all good writing begins with terrible first efforts. You need to start somewhere. Start by getting something—anything—down on paper. A friend of mine says that the first draft is the down draft—you just get it down. The second draft is the up draft—you fix it up. You try to say what you have to say more accurately. And the third draft is the dental draft, where you check every tooth, to see if it's loose or cramped or decayed, or even, God help us, healthy.

What I've learned to do when I sit down to work on a shitty first draft is to quiet the voices in my head. First there's the vinegar-lipped Reader Lady, who says primly, "Well, that's not very interesting, is it?" And there's the emaciated German male who writes these Orwellian memos detailing your thought crimes. And there are your parents, agonizing over your lack of loyalty and discretion; and there's William Burroughs, dozing off or shooting up because he finds you as bold and articulate as a houseplant; and so on. And there are also the dogs; let's not forget the dogs, the dogs in their pen who will surely hurtle and snarl their way out if you ever stop writing, because writing is, for some of us, the latch that keeps the door of the pen closed, keeps those crazy ravenous dogs contained.

Quieting those voices is at least half the battle I fight daily. But this is better than it used to be. It used to be 87 percent. Left to its own devices, my mind spends much of its time having conversations with people who aren't there. I walk along defending myself to people, or exchanging repartee with them, or rationalizing my behavior, or seducing them with gossip, or pretending I'm on their TV talk show or whatever. I speed or run an aging yellow light or don't come to a full stop, and one nanosecond later am explaining to imaginary cops exactly why I had to do what I did, or insisting that I did not in fact do it.

I happened to mention this to a hypnotist I saw many years ago, and he looked at me very nicely. At first I thought he was feeling around on the floor for the silent alarm button, but then he gave me the following exercise, which I still use to this day. Close your eyes and get quiet for a minute, until the chatter starts up. Then isolate one of the voices and imagine the person speaking as a mouse. Pick it up by the tail and drop it into a mason jar. Then isolate another voice, pick it up by the tail, drop it in the jar. And so on. Drop in any high-maintenance parental units, drop in any contractors, lawyers, colleagues, children, anyone who is whining in your head. Then put the lid on, and watch all these mouse people clawing at the glass, jabbering away, trying to make you feel like shit because you won't do what they want—won't give them more money, won't be more successful, won't see them more often. Then imagine that there is a volume-control button on the bottle. Turn it all the way up for a moment, and listen to the stream of angry, neglected, guilt-mongering voices. Then turn it all the way down and watch the frantic mice lunge at the glass, trying to get to you. Leave it down, and get back to your shitty first draft.

A writer friend of mine suggests opening the jar and shooting them all in the head. But I think he's a little angry, and I'm sure nothing like this would ever occur to you.

## Content

1. Based on the definitions provided in "Chapter 3: Academic Writing," how is Lamott's drafting process similar to brainstorming or freewriting? What (if anything) distinguishes drafting from freewriting?

2. How does anxiety hinder the writing process? What advice does Lamott offer for combating anxiety?

3. Who are the voices that haunt Lamott while she writes? What voices or self-doubts do you experience when writing?

## Craft

1. What is Lamott's thesis? Is the thesis clearly stated or implied?

2. Do Lamott's anecdotes about her reviewing days enhance her message or distract from it?

3. Why are some of Lamott's paragraphs very short while others are quite long? Are these paragraphs organized effectively?

4. What is Lamott's tone? Explain your answer using details from the text. How does this tone help Lamott achieve her purpose of helping other writers?

## Contemplation

1. What writing advice have you been given throughout your educational career? Was this advice helpful or discouraging? Have you ever received contradictory advice or instruction? How did you decide which advice to follow?

# Simplicity

## by William Zinsser

*William Zinsser began his writing career in 1946 as a writer and editor for the*
New York Herald Tribune. *During the 1970s, Zinsser taught at Yale University
and published his iconic writing manual,* On Writing Well. *His other books
contemplate topics ranging from jazz music to baseball and genres from travel-
writing to memoir. In 2011 his weekly blog* Zinsser on Friday *won The National
Magazine Award for digital media. The blog was compiled into* The Writer Who
Stayed, *a book whose title hints at Zinsser's decades-long role as a scholar with
one foot in academia and one foot in popular culture.*

Clutter is the disease of American writing. We are a society strangling in
unnecessary words, circular constructions, pompous frills and meaningless
jargon.

Who can understand the viscous language of everyday American commerce
and enterprise: the business letter, the interoffice memo, the corporation
report, the notice from the bank explaining its latest "simplified"
statement? What member of an insurance or medical plan can decipher
the brochure that tells him what his costs and benefits are? What father
or mother can put together a child's toy—on Christmas Eve or any other
eve—from the instructions on the box? Our national tendency is to inflate
and thereby sound important. The airline pilot who announces that he is
presently anticipating experiencing considerable precipitation wouldn't
dream of saying that it may rain. The sentence is too simple—there must be
something wrong with it.

But the secret of good writing is to strip every sentence to its cleanest
components. Every word that serves no function, every long word that
could be a short word, every adverb that carries the same meaning that's
already in the verb, every passive construction that leaves the reader unsure
of who is doing what—these are the thousand and one adulterants that
weaken the strength of a sentence. And they usually occur, ironically, in
proportion to education and rank.

During the late 1960s the president of a major university wrote a letter to
mollify the alumni after a spell of campus unrest. "You are probably aware,"
he began, "that we have been experiencing very considerable potentially
explosive expressions of dissatisfaction on issues only partially related."
He meant that the students had been hassling them about different

Zinsser, William. "Simplicity." *On Writing Well: The Classic Guide to Writing Nonfiction.* 2nd ed. New York:
Harper & Row, 1980. 6-11. Rpt. in *Decorum.* Ed. Kristina Gladfelter and Melody Niesen. Revised
2nd ed. Southlake, TX: Fountainhead, 2016. 130-133. Print.

things. I was far more upset by the president's English than by the students' potentially explosive expressions of dissatisfaction. I would have preferred the presidential approach taken by Franklin D. Roosevelt when he tried to convert into English his own government's memos, such as this blackout order of 1942:

Such preparations shall be made as will completely obscure all Federal buildings and non-Federal buildings occupied by the Federal government during an air raid for any period of time from visibility by reason of internal or external illumination.

"Tell them," Roosevelt said, "that in buildings where they have to keep the work going to put something across the windows."

Simplify, simplify. Thoreau said it, as we are so often reminded, and no American writer more consistently practiced what he preached. Open Walden to any page and you will find a man saying in a plain and orderly way what is on his mind:

> I love to be alone. I never found the companion that was so companionable as solitude. We are for the most part more lonely when we go abroad among men than when we stay in our chambers. A man thinking or working is always alone, let him be where he will. Solitude is not measured by the miles of space that intervene between a man and his fellows. The really diligent student in one of the crowded hives of Cambridge College is as solitary as a dervish in the desert.

How can the rest of us achieve such enviable freedom from clutter? The answer is to clear our heads of clutter. Clear thinking becomes clear writing: one can't exist without the other. It is impossible for a muddy thinker to write good English. He may get away with it for a paragraph or two, but soon the reader will be lost, and there is no sin so grave, for he will not easily be lured back.

Who is this elusive creature the reader? He is a person with an attention span of about twenty seconds. He is assailed on every side by forces competing for his time: by newspapers and magazines, by television and radio, by his stereo and videocassettes, by his wife and children and pets, by his house and his yard and all the gadgets that he has bought to keep them spruce, and by that most potent of competitors, sleep. The man snoozing in his chair with an unfinished magazine open on his lap is a man who was being given too much unnecessary trouble by the writer.

It won't do to say that the snoozing reader is too dumb or too lazy to keep pace with the train of thought. My sympathies are with him. If the reader is lost, it is generally because the writer has not been careful enough to keep him on the path.

This carelessness can take any number of forms. Perhaps a sentence is so excessively cluttered that the reader, hacking his way through the verbiage, simply doesn't know what it means. Perhaps a sentence has been so shoddily constructed that the reader could read it in any of several ways. Perhaps the writer has switched pronouns in mid-sentence, or has switched tenses, so the reader loses track of who is talking or when the action took place. Perhaps Sentence B is not a logical sequel to Sentence A—the writer, in whose head the connection is clear, has not bothered to provide the missing link. Perhaps the writer has used an important word incorrectly by not taking the trouble to look it up. He may think that "sanguine" and "sanguinary" mean the same thing, but the difference is a bloody big one. The reader can only infer (speaking of big differences) what the writer is trying to imply.

Faced with these obstacles, the reader is at first a remarkably tenacious bird. He blames himself—he obviously missed something, and he goes back over the mystifying sentence, or over the whole paragraph, piecing it out like an ancient rune, making guesses and moving on. But he won't do this for long. The writer is making him work too hard, and the reader will look for one who is better at his craft. The writer must therefore constantly ask himself: What am I trying to say? Surprisingly often, he doesn't know. Then he must look at what he has written and ask: Have I said it? Is it clear to someone encountering the subject for the first time? If it's not, it is because some fuzz has worked its way into the machinery. The clear writer is a person clear-headed enough to see this stuff for what it is: fuzz.

I don't mean that some people are born clear-headed and are therefore natural writers, whereas others are naturally fuzzy and will never write well. Thinking clearly is a conscious act that the writer must force upon himself, just as if he were embarking on any other project that requires logic: adding up a laundry list or doing an algebra problem. Good writing doesn't come naturally, though most people obviously think it does. The professional writer is forever being bearded by strangers who say that they'd like to "try a little writing sometime" when they retire from their real profession. Or they say, "I could write a book about that." I doubt it.

Writing is hard work. A clear sentence is no accident. Very few sentences come out right the first time, or even the third time. Remember this as a consolation in moments of despair. If you find that writing is hard, it's because it is hard. It's one of the hardest things that people do.

## Content

1. According to Zinsser, why do Americans tend to inflate their language?

2. How does Zinsser define "clutter?" Why is clutter a problem?

3. What advice does Zinsser offer for writers trying to avoid clutter?

4. What is the relationship between clear thinking and clear writing?

## Craft

1. Zinsser includes a number of examples of cluttered writing. Which example struck you as most effective?

2. Does Zinsser follow his own advice? Use specific word choices and sentences to support your answer.

3. Zinsser covers three main topics: cluttered writing, readers, and writers. What transitional phrases does Zinsser use to move from one topic to the next?

## Contemplation

1. Zinsser proposes, "We are a society strangling in unnecessary words, circular constructions, pompous frills and meaningless jargon." Have you noticed this tendency in your writing or the writing of others? Why might you write in a way that could be considered "cluttered"? As you consider these questions, are there any circumstances when cluttered writing is appropriate? How can writers balance the advice to use "formal speech" with Zinsser's advice to write simply?

# The Shadow Scholar

## by Ed Dante

## The man who writes your students' papers tells his story

*Ed Dante is a pseudonym for a writer who lives on the East Coast. Through a literary agent, he approached* The Chronicle *wanting to tell the story of how he makes a living writing papers for a custom-essay company and to describe the extent of student cheating he has observed. In the course of editing his article,* The Chronicle *reviewed correspondence Dante had with clients and some of the papers he had been paid to write. In the article published here, some details of the assignment he describes have been altered to protect the identity of the student.*

The request came in by e-mail around 2 in the afternoon. It was from a previous customer, and she had urgent business. I quote her message here verbatim (if I had to put up with it, so should you): "You did me business ethics propsal for me I need propsal got approved pls can you will write me paper?"

I've gotten pretty good at interpreting this kind of correspondence. The client had attached a document from her professor with details about the paper. She needed the first section in a week. Seventy-five pages.

I told her no problem.

It truly was no problem. In the past year, I've written roughly 5,000 pages of scholarly literature, most on very tight deadlines. But you won't find my name on a single paper.

I've written toward a master's degree in cognitive psychology, a Ph.D. in sociology, and a handful of postgraduate credits in international diplomacy. I've worked on bachelor's degrees in hospitality, business administration, and accounting. I've written for courses in history, cinema, labor relations, pharmacology, theology, sports management, maritime security, airline services, sustainability, municipal budgeting, marketing, philosophy, ethics, Eastern religion, postmodern architecture, anthropology, literature, and public administration. I've attended three dozen online universities. I've completed 12 graduate theses of 50 pages or more. All for someone else.

You've never heard of me, but there's a good chance that you've read some of my work. I'm a hired gun, a doctor of everything, an academic mercenary.

Dante, Ed. "The Shadow Scholar." *The Chronicle of Higher Education*. The Chronicle of Higher Education, 2010. Web. 27 May 2016. Rpt. in *Decorum*. Ed. Kristina Gladfelter and Melody Niesen. Revised 2nd ed. Southlake, TX: Fountainhead, 2016. 134-143. Print.

My customers are your students. I promise you that. Somebody in your classroom uses a service that you can't detect, that you can't defend against, that you may not even know exists.

I work at an online company that generates tens of thousands of dollars a month by creating original essays based on specific instructions provided by cheating students. I've worked there full time since 2004. On any day of the academic year, I am working on upward of 20 assignments.

In the midst of this great recession, business is booming. At busy times, during midterms and finals, my company's staff of roughly 50 writers is not large enough to satisfy the demands of students who will pay for our work and claim it as their own.

You would be amazed by the incompetence of your students' writing. I have seen the word "desperate" misspelled every way you can imagine. And these students truly are desperate. They couldn't write a convincing grocery list, yet they are in graduate school. They really need help. They need help learning and, separately, they need help passing their courses. But they aren't getting it.

For those of you who have ever mentored a student through the writing of a dissertation, served on a thesis-review committee, or guided a graduate student through a formal research process, I have a question: Do you ever wonder how a student who struggles to formulate complete sentences in conversation manages to produce marginally competent research? How does that student get by you?

I live well on the desperation, misery, and incompetence that your educational system has created. Granted, as a writer, I could earn more; certainly there are ways to earn less. But I never struggle to find work. And as my peers trudge through thankless office jobs that seem more intolerable with every passing month of our sustained recession, I am on pace for my best year yet. I will make roughly $66,000 this year. Not a king's ransom, but higher than what many actual educators are paid.

Of course, I know you are aware that cheating occurs. But you have no idea how deeply this kind of cheating penetrates the academic system, much less how to stop it. Last summer *The New York Times* reported that 61 percent of undergraduates have admitted to some form of cheating on assignments and exams. Yet there is little discussion about custom papers and how they differ from more-detectable forms of plagiarism, or about why students cheat in the first place.

It is my hope that this essay will initiate such a conversation. As for me, I'm planning to retire. I'm tired of helping you make your students look competent.

It is late in the semester when the business student contacts me, a time when I typically juggle deadlines and push out 20 to 40 pages a day. I had written a short research proposal for her a few weeks before, suggesting a project that connected a surge of unethical business practices to the patterns of trade liberalization. The proposal was approved, and now I had six days to complete the assignment. This was not quite a rush order, which we get top dollar to write. This assignment would be priced at a standard $2,000, half of which goes in my pocket.

A few hours after I had agreed to write the paper, I received the following e-mail: "sending sorces for ur to use thanx."

I did not reply immediately. One hour later, I received another message:

"did u get the sorce I send

please where you are now?

Desprit to pass spring projict"

Not only was this student going to be a constant thorn in my side, but she also communicated in haiku, each less decipherable than the one before it. I let her know that I was giving her work the utmost attention, that I had received her sources, and that I would be in touch if I had any questions. Then I put it aside.

From my experience, three demographic groups seek out my services: the English-as-second-language student; the hopelessly deficient student; and the lazy rich kid.

For the last, colleges are a perfect launching ground—they are built to reward the rich and to forgive them their laziness. Let's be honest: The successful among us are not always the best and the brightest, and certainly not the most ethical. My favorite customers are those with an unlimited supply of money and no shortage of instructions on how they would like to see their work executed. While the deficient student will generally not know how to ask for what he wants until he doesn't get it, the lazy rich student will know exactly what he wants. He is poised for a life of paying others and telling them what to do. Indeed, he is acquiring all the skills he needs to stay on top.

As for the first two types of students—the ESL and the hopelessly deficient—colleges are utterly failing them. Students who come to American universities from other countries find that their efforts to learn a new language are confounded not only by cultural difficulties but also by the pressures of grading. The focus on evaluation rather than education means that those who haven't mastered English must do so quickly or suffer the consequences. My service provides a particularly quick way to "master" English. And those who are hopelessly deficient—a euphemism, I admit—struggle with communication in general.

Two days had passed since I last heard from the business student. Overnight I had received 14 e-mails from her. She had additional instructions for the assignment, such as "but more again please make sure they are a good link betwee the leticture review and all the chapter and the benfet of my paper. finally do you think the level of this work? how match i can get it?"

I'll admit, I didn't fully understand that one.

It was followed by some clarification: "where u are can you get my messages? Please I pay a lot and dont have ao to faile I strated to get very worry."

Her messages had arrived between 2 a.m. and 6 a.m. Again I assured her I had the matter under control.

It was true. At this point, there are few academic challenges that I find intimidating. You name it, I've been paid to write about it.

Customers' orders are endlessly different yet strangely all the same. No matter what the subject, clients want to be assured that their assignment is in capable hands. It would be terrible to think that your Ivy League graduate thesis was riding on the work ethic and perspicacity of a public-university slacker. So part of my job is to be whatever my clients want me to be. I say yes when I am asked if I have a Ph.D. in sociology. I say yes when I am asked if I have professional training in industrial/organizational psychology. I say yes when asked if I have ever designed a perpetual-motion-powered time machine and documented my efforts in a peer-reviewed journal.

The subject matter, the grade level, the college, the course—these things are irrelevant to me. Prices are determined per page and are based on how long I have to complete the assignment. As long as it doesn't require me to do any math or video-documented animal husbandry, I will write anything.

I have completed countless online courses. Students provide me with passwords and user names so I can access key documents and online exams. In some instances, I have even contributed to weekly online discussions with other students in the class.

I have become a master of the admissions essay. I have written these for undergraduate, master's, and doctoral programs, some at elite universities. I can explain exactly why you're Brown material, why the Wharton M.B.A. program would benefit from your presence, how certain life experiences have prepared you for the rigors of your chosen course of study. I do not mean to be insensitive, but I can't tell you how many times I've been paid to write about somebody helping a loved one battle cancer. I've written essays that could be adapted into Meryl Streep movies.

I do a lot of work for seminary students. I like seminary students. They seem so blissfully unaware of the inherent contradiction in paying somebody to help them cheat in courses that are largely about walking in the light of God and providing an ethical model for others to follow. I have been commissioned to write many a passionate condemnation of America's moral decay as exemplified by abortion, gay marriage, or the teaching of evolution. All in all, we may presume that clerical authorities see these as a greater threat than the plagiarism committed by the future frocked.

With respect to America's nurses, fear not. Our lives are in capable hands— just hands that can't write a lick. Nursing students account for one of my company's biggest customer bases. I've written case-management plans, reports on nursing ethics, and essays on why nurse practitioners are lighting the way to the future of medicine. I've even written pharmaceutical-treatment courses, for patients who I hope were hypothetical.

I, who have no name, no opinions, and no style, have written so many papers at this point, including legal briefs, military-strategy assessments, poems, lab reports, and, yes, even papers on academic integrity, that it's hard to determine which course of study is most infested with cheating. But I'd say education is the worst. I've written papers for students in elementary-education programs, special-education majors, and ESL-training courses. I've written lesson plans for aspiring high-school teachers, and I've synthesized reports from notes that customers have taken during classroom observations. I've written essays for those studying to become school administrators, and I've completed theses for those on course to become principals. In the enormous conspiracy that is student cheating, the frontline intelligence community is infiltrated by double agents. (Future educators of America, I know who you are.)

As the deadline for the business-ethics paper approaches, I think about what's ahead of me. Whenever I take on an assignment this large, I get a certain physical sensation. My body says: Are you sure you want to do this again? You know how much it hurt the last time. You know this student will be with you for a long time. You know you will become her emergency contact, her guidance counselor and life raft. You know that for the 48 hours that you dedicate to writing this paper, you will cease all human functions but typing, you will Google until the term has lost all meaning, and you will drink enough coffee to fuel a revolution in a small Central American country.

But then there's the money, the sense that I must capitalize on opportunity, and even a bit of a thrill in seeing whether I can do it.

And I can. It's not implausible to write a 75-page paper in two days. It's just miserable. I don't need much sleep, and when I get cranking, I can churn out four or five pages an hour. First I lay out the sections of an assignment—introduction, problem statement, methodology, literature review, findings, conclusion—whatever the instructions call for. Then I start Googling.

I haven't been to a library once since I started doing this job. Amazon is quite generous about free samples. If I can find a single page from a particular text, I can cobble that into a report, deducing what I don't know from customer reviews and publisher blurbs. Google Scholar is a great source for material, providing the abstract of nearly any journal article. And of course, there's Wikipedia, which is often my first stop when dealing with unfamiliar subjects. Naturally one must verify such material elsewhere, but I've taken hundreds of crash courses this way.

After I've gathered my sources, I pull out usable quotes, cite them, and distribute them among the sections of the assignment. Over the years, I've refined ways of stretching papers. I can write a four-word sentence in 40 words. Just give me one phrase of quotable text, and I'll produce two pages of ponderous explanation. I can say in 10 pages what most normal people could say in a paragraph.

I've also got a mental library of stock academic phrases: "A close consideration of the events which occurred in ____ during the ____ demonstrate that ____ had entered into a phase of widespread cultural, social, and economic change that would define ____ for decades to come." Fill in the blanks using words provided by the professor in the assignment's instructions.

How good is the product created by this process? That depends—on the day, my mood, how many other assignments I am working on. It also depends on the customer, his or her expectations, and the degree to which the completed work exceeds his or her abilities. I don't ever edit my assignments. That way I get fewer customer requests to "dumb it down." So some of my work is great. Some of it is not so great. Most of my clients do not have the wherewithal to tell the difference, which probably means that in most cases the work is better than what the student would have produced on his or her own. I've actually had customers thank me for being clever enough to insert typos. "Nice touch," they'll say.

I've read enough academic material to know that I'm not the only bullshit artist out there. I think about how Dickens got paid per word and how, as a result, *Bleak House* is … well, let's be diplomatic and say exhaustive. Dickens is a role model for me.

So how does someone become a custom-paper writer? The story of how I got into this job may be instructive. It is mostly about the tremendous disappointment that awaited me in college.

My distaste for the early hours and regimented nature of high school was tempered by the promise of the educational community ahead, with its free exchange of ideas and access to great minds. How dispiriting to find out that college was just another place where grades were grubbed, competition overshadowed personal growth, and the threat of failure was used to encourage learning.

Although my university experience did not live up to its vaunted reputation, it did lead me to where I am today. I was raised in an upper-middle-class family, but I went to college in a poor neighborhood. I fit in really well: After paying my tuition, I didn't have a cent to my name. I had nothing but a meal plan and my roommate's computer. But I was determined to write for a living, and, moreover, to spend these extremely expensive years learning how to do so. When I completed my first novel, in the summer between sophomore and junior years, I contacted the English department about creating an independent study around editing and publishing it. I was received like a mental patient. I was told, "There's nothing like that here." I was told that I could go back to my classes, sit in my lectures, and fill out Scantron tests until I graduated.

I didn't much care for my classes, though. I slept late and spent the afternoons working on my own material. Then a funny thing happened. Here I was, begging anybody in authority to take my work seriously. But my classmates did. They saw my abilities and my abundance of free time. They saw a value that the university did not.

It turned out that my lazy, Xanax-snorting, Miller-swilling classmates were thrilled to pay me to write their papers. And I was thrilled to take their money. Imagine you are crumbling under the weight of university-issued parking tickets and self-doubt when a frat boy offers you cash to write about Plato. Doing that job was a no-brainer. Word of my services spread quickly, especially through the fraternities. Soon I was receiving calls from strangers who wanted to commission my work. I was a writer!

Nearly a decade later, students, not publishers, still come from everywhere to find me.

I work hard for a living. I'm nice to people. But I understand that in simple terms, I'm the bad guy. I see where I'm vulnerable to ethical scrutiny.

But pointing the finger at me is too easy. Why does my business thrive? Why do so many students prefer to cheat rather than do their own work?

Say what you want about me, but I am not the reason your students cheat.

You know what's never happened? I've never had a client complain that he'd been expelled from school, that the originality of his work had been questioned, that some disciplinary action had been taken. As far as I know, not one of my customers has ever been caught.

With just two days to go, I was finally ready to throw myself into the business assignment. I turned off my phone, caged myself in my office, and went through the purgatory of cramming the summation of a student's alleged education into a weekend. Try it sometime. After the 20th hour on a single subject, you have an almost-out-of-body experience.

My client was thrilled with my work. She told me that she would present the chapter to her mentor and get back to me with our next steps. Two weeks passed, by which time the assignment was but a distant memory, obscured by the several hundred pages I had written since. On a Wednesday evening, I received the following e-mail:

"Thanx u so much for the chapter is going very good the porfesser likes it but wants the folloing suggestions please what do you thing?:

"'The hypothesis is interesting but I'd like to see it a bit more focused. Choose a specific connection and try to prove it.'

"What shoudwe say?"

This happens a lot. I get paid per assignment. But with longer papers, the student starts to think of me as a personal educational counselor. She paid me to write a one-page response to her professor, and then she paid me to revise her paper. I completed each of these assignments, sustaining the voice that the student had established and maintaining the front of competence from some invisible location far beneath the ivory tower.

The 75-page paper on business ethics ultimately expanded into a 160-page graduate thesis, every word of which was written by me. I can't remember the name of my client, but it's her name on my work. We collaborated for months. As with so many other topics I tackle, the connection between unethical business practices and trade liberalization became a subtext to my everyday life.

So, of course, you can imagine my excitement when I received the good news:

"thanx so much for uhelp ican going to graduate to now".

## Content

1. Ed Dante states he can write a seventy-five page paper in two days. What is his writing process?

2. Who are Dante's most frequent clients? Why do they choose to purchase papers?

3. How did Dante begin writing other people's papers?

4. Who does Dante blame for the student's widespread cheating and plagiarism? Use details from the text to support all of your answers.

## Craft

1. Why does Dante include excerpts from his client's e-mails? Is this an effective strategy? Why or why not?

2. According to Dante, what is his purpose for publishing this essay? Does the content of the essay itself support this purpose? Explain using details from the text.

3. How does Dante establish ethos throughout the essay? Given his role as an "academic mercenary," how credible are his claims

about the college educational system? Why is Dante's credibility important to consider?

## Contemplation

1. Dante's essay paints a grim picture of college education where "lazy, Xanax-snorting classmates were thrilled to pay me to write their papers" and teachers are "utterly failing" ESL students. How accurate is Dante's description? If the situation is as hopeless as Dante claims, are students justified in cheating? Is cheating more acceptable for some students? Are there any examples of cheating that you found more troubling than others?

---

### Assignment

#### Write an Interview

Dante uses "you" throughout his essay to address teachers. For example, he writes, "I live well on the desperation, misery, and incompetence that your education system has created." Pick one or two claims that Dante makes about college education or teachers. Then compile a list of 4 to 6/ questions about the topic. Use your questions to interview a teacher, administrator, or advisor. It may be useful to explain the context of the questions and Dante's essay during your interview. Afterward, use the interview answers to write a short paper responding to Dante's essay.

# Superman and Me

## by Sherman Alexie

*Poet, novelist, and filmmaker Sherman Alexie grew up on the Spokane Indian Reservation in Wellpinit, Washington. Alexie's Spokane childhood inspired the National Book Award winning* Absolutely True Diary of a Part-Time Indian. *In* Absolutely True Diary, *as well as in his poetry and novels for adults, Alexie combines dark humor and brutal realism to explore the complexities of Native American life. His writing has won numerous awards including the PEN/ Hemingway Award for* The Lone Ranger and Tonto Fistfight in Heaven, *the American Book Award for* Reservation Blues, *and the Native Writers' Circle Lifetime Achievement Award. In addition to writing, Alexie is an outspoken supporter of Native American film makers and independent bookstores.*

I learned to read with a Superman comic book. Simple enough, I suppose. I cannot recall which particular Superman comic book I read, nor can I remember which villain he fought in that issue. I cannot remember the plot, nor the means by which I obtained the comic book. What I can remember is this: I was 3 years old, a Spokane Indian boy living with his family on the Spokane Indian Reservation in eastern Washington state. We were poor by most standards, but one of my parents usually managed to find some minimum-wage job or another, which made us middle-class by reservation standards. I had a brother and three sisters. We lived on a combination of irregular paychecks, hope, fear and government surplus food.

My father, who is one of the few Indians who went to Catholic school on purpose, was an avid reader of westerns, spy thrillers, murder mysteries, gangster epics, basketball player biographies and anything else he could find. He bought his books by the pound at Dutch's Pawn Shop, Goodwill, Salvation Army and Value Village. When he had extra money, he bought new novels at supermarkets, convenience stores and hospital gift shops. Our house was filled with books. They were stacked in crazy piles in the bathroom, bedrooms and living room. In a fit of unemployment-inspired creative energy, my father built a set of bookshelves and soon filled them with a random assortment of books about the Kennedy assassination, Watergate, the Vietnam War and the entire 23-book series of the Apache westerns. My father loved books, and since I loved my father with an aching devotion, I decided to love books as well.

Alexie, Sherman. "Superman and Me." *The Most Wonderful Books: Writers on Discovering the Pleasures of Reading.* 1st ed. Ed. Michael Dorris and Emilie Buchwald. Minneapolis: Milkweed, 1998. Rpt. in *Decorum.* Ed. Kristina Gladfelter and Melody Niesen. Revised 2nd ed. Southlake, TX: Fountainhead, 2016. 144-146. Print.

I can remember picking up my father's books before I could read. The words themselves were mostly foreign, but I still remember the exact moment when I first understood, with a sudden clarity, the purpose of a paragraph. I didn't have the vocabulary to say "paragraph," but I realized that a paragraph was a fence that held words. The words inside a paragraph worked together for a common purpose. They had some specific reason for being inside the same fence. This knowledge delighted me. I began to think of everything in terms of paragraphs. Our reservation was a small paragraph within the United States. My family's house was a paragraph, distinct from the other paragraphs of the LeBrets to the north, the Fords to our south and the Tribal School to the west. Inside our house, each family member existed as a separate paragraph but still had genetics and common experiences to link us. Now, using this logic, I can see my changed family as an essay of seven paragraphs: mother, father, older brother, the deceased sister, my younger twin sisters and our adopted little brother.

At the same time I was seeing the world in paragraphs, I also picked up that Superman comic book. Each panel, complete with picture, dialogue and narrative was a three-dimensional paragraph. In one panel, Superman breaks through a door. His suit is red, blue and yellow. The brown door shatters into many pieces. I look at the narrative above the picture. I cannot read the words, but I assume it tells me that "Superman is breaking down the door." Aloud, I pretend to read the words and say, "Superman is breaking down the door." Words, dialogue, also float out of Superman's mouth. Because he is breaking down the door, I assume he says, "I am breaking down the door." Once again, I pretend to read the words and say aloud, "I am breaking down the door." In this way, I learned to read.

This might be an interesting story all by itself. A little Indian boy teaches himself to read at an early age and advances quickly. He reads "Grapes of Wrath" in kindergarten when other children are struggling through "Dick and Jane." If he'd been anything but an Indian boy living on the reservation, he might have been called a prodigy. But he is an Indian boy living on the reservation and is simply an oddity. He grows into a man who often speaks of his childhood in the third-person, as if it will somehow dull the pain and make him sound more modest about his talents.

A smart Indian is a dangerous person, widely feared and ridiculed by Indians and non-Indians alike. I fought with my classmates on a daily basis. They wanted me to stay quiet when the non-Indian teacher asked for answers, for volunteers, for help. We were Indian children who were expected to be stupid. Most lived up to those expectations inside the classroom but subverted them on the outside. They struggled with basic reading in school but could remember how to sing a few dozen powwow songs. They were monosyllabic in front of their non-Indian teachers but could tell complicated stories and jokes at the dinner table. They submissively ducked their heads when confronted by a non-Indian adult but would slug it out with the Indian bully who was 10 years older. As Indian children, we were expected to fail in the non-Indian world. Those who failed were ceremonially accepted by other Indians and appropriately pitied by non-Indians.

I refused to fail. I was smart. I was arrogant. I was lucky. I read books late into the night, until I could barely keep my eyes open. I read books at recess, then during lunch, and in the few minutes left after I had finished my classroom assignments. I read books in the car when my family traveled to powwows or basketball games. In shopping malls, I ran to the bookstores and read bits and pieces of as many books as I could. I read books my father brought home from the pawnshops and secondhand. I read the books I borrowed from the library. I read the backs of cereal boxes. I read the newspaper. I read the bulletins posted on the walls of the school, the clinic, the tribal offices, the post office. I read junk mail. I read auto-repair manuals. I read magazines. I read anything that had words and paragraphs. I read with equal parts joy and desperation. I loved those books, but I also knew that love had only one purpose. I was trying to save my life.

Despite all the books I read, I am still surprised I became a writer. I was going to be a pediatrician. These days, I write novels, short stories, and poems. I visit schools and teach creative writing to Indian kids. In all my years in the reservation school system, I was never taught how to write poetry, short stories or novels. I was certainly never taught that Indians wrote poetry, short stories and novels. Writing was something beyond Indians. I cannot recall a single time that a guest teacher visited the reservation. There must have been visiting teachers. Who were they? Where are they now? Do they exist? I visit the schools as often as possible. The Indian kids crowd the classroom. Many are writing their own poems, short stories and novels. They have read my books. They have read many other books. They look at me with bright eyes and arrogant wonder. They are trying to save their lives. Then there are the sullen and already defeated Indian kids who sit in the back rows and ignore me with theatrical precision. The pages of their notebooks are empty. They carry neither pencil nor pen. They stare out the window. They refuse to resist. "Books," I say to them. "Books," I say. I throw my weight against their locked doors. The door holds. I am smart. I am arrogant. I am lucky. I am trying to save our lives.

## Content

1. How did Alexie learn to read? Why did he "decide" to love books?

2. According to Alexie, what is a paragraph? How is Alexie's explanation similar or different than the one provided in your textbook's discussion of paragraphs?

3. How was Alexie different than his classmates? How was his family different than other families on the Spokane Indian Reservation? What inferences can you make about reservation life based on these descriptions?

4. Why does Alexie claim "a smart Indian is a dangerous person?" How do the attitudes of his teachers and classmates support his claim?

## Craft

1. What is Alexie's tone? How does it change throughout the essay? Find a sentence or two that illustrate Alexie's tone.

2. How does Alexie use repetition in the essay?

3. In his final sentence, Alexie writes, "I am trying to save **our** lives" as he describes trying to connect with Native American students. How would the meaning of the sentence change if he wrote "their lives?" Why do you think Alexie chose "our" instead of "their?"

## Contemplation

1. Alexie writes, "We were Indian children who were expected to be stupid. Most lived up to those expectations inside the classroom but subverted them on the outside." Alexie's description of the divide between native student and their non-native teachers hints at a long conflict between Native Americans and outside educators. From the mid-1800s onward, many Native American children were forcibly taken away from their families and placed in boarding schools. These schools operated under the motto, "Kill the Indian; save the child." While some boarding schools provided a solid Western education, many were more like work houses than schools. Native children were forbidden from speaking their tribal languages, given new names, and punished for practicing their culture.

   Though Alexie was a generation removed from this experience, it nonetheless provides an important context for interpreting the educational environment Alexie describes. Given this context, why might native students be reluctant to participate in class? Do you think their strategy helped or harmed them? How do students (from all backgrounds) subvert the classrooms? Why do they disengage and what should teachers do to earn their trust and attention?

# Is Google Making Us Stupid?

## by Nicholas Carr

*Nicholas Carr graduated from Dartmouth College and Harvard University where he later served as executive editor of the* Harvard Business Review. *In 2008, he served on the Editorial Board of Advisors of Encyclopedia Britannica. In his books and essays, Carr wrangles with the opportunities and consequences of America's technology-driven society. The following essay was published by* The Atlantic *as the cover story of its annual Idea issue. The essay ignited heated debate and remains a touch-stone in the academic conversation about technology's social and cognitive consequences.*

## What the Internet is doing to our brains

"Dave, stop. Stop, will you? Stop, Dave. Will you stop, Dave?" So the supercomputer HAL pleads with the implacable astronaut Dave Bowman in a famous and weirdly poignant scene toward the end of Stanley Kubrick's *2001: A Space Odyssey*. Bowman, having nearly been sent to a deep-space death by the malfunctioning machine, is calmly, coldly disconnecting the memory circuits that control its artificial "brain. "Dave, my mind is going," HAL says, forlornly. "I can feel it. I can feel it."

I can feel it, too. Over the past few years I've had an uncomfortable sense that someone, or something, has been tinkering with my brain, remapping the neural circuitry, reprogramming the memory. My mind isn't going— so far as I can tell—but it's changing. I'm not thinking the way I used to think. I can feel it most strongly when I'm reading. Immersing myself in a book or a lengthy article used to be easy. My mind would get caught up in the narrative or the turns of the argument, and I'd spend hours strolling through long stretches of prose. That's rarely the case anymore. Now my concentration often starts to drift after two or three pages. I get fidgety, lose the thread, begin looking for something else to do. I feel as if I'm always dragging my wayward brain back to the text. The deep reading that used to come naturally has become a struggle.

I think I know what's going on. For more than a decade now, I've been spending a lot of time online, searching and surfing and sometimes adding to the great databases of the Internet. The Web has been a godsend to me as a writer. Research that once required days in the stacks or periodical rooms of libraries can now be done in minutes. A few Google searches, some

Carr, Nicholas. "Is Google Making Us Stupid?" *The Atlantic*. Atlantic Media Company, July/August 2008. Web. 27 May 2016. Rpt. in *Decorum*. Ed. Kristina Gladfelter and Melody Niesen. Revised 2nd ed. Southlake, TX: Fountainhead, 2016. 149-158. Print.

quick clicks on hyperlinks, and I've got the telltale fact or pithy quote I was after. Even when I'm not working, I'm as likely as not to be foraging in the Web's info-thickets reading and writing e-mails, scanning headlines and blog posts, watching videos and listening to podcasts, or just tripping from link to link to link. (Unlike footnotes, to which they're sometimes likened, hyperlinks don't merely point to related works; they propel you toward them.)

For me, as for others, the Net is becoming a universal medium, the conduit for most of the information that flows through my eyes and ears and into my mind. The advantages of having immediate access to such an incredibly rich store of information are many, and they've been widely described and duly applauded. "The perfect recall of silicon memory," *Wired's* Clive Thompson has written, "can be an enormous boon to thinking." But that boon comes at a price. As the media theorist Marshall McLuhan pointed out in the 1960s, media are not just passive channels of information. They supply the stuff of thought, but they also shape the process of thought. And what the Net seems to be doing is chipping away my capacity for concentration and contemplation. My mind now expects to take in information the way the Net distributes it: in a swiftly moving stream of particles. Once I was a scuba diver in the sea of words. Now I zip along the surface like a guy on a Jet Ski.

I'm not the only one. When I mention my troubles with reading to friends and acquaintances—literary types, most of them—many say they're having similar experiences. The more they use the Web, the more they have to fight to stay focused on long pieces of writing. Some of the bloggers I follow have also begun mentioning the phenomenon. Scott Karp, who writes a blog about online media, recently confessed that he has stopped reading books altogether. "I was a lit major in college, and used to be [a] voracious book reader," he wrote. "What happened?" He speculates on the answer: "What if I do all my reading on the web not so much because the way I read has changed, i.e. I'm just seeking convenience, but because the way I THINK has changed?"

Bruce Friedman, who blogs regularly about the use of computers in medicine, also has described how the Internet has altered his mental habits. "I now have almost totally lost the ability to read and absorb a longish article on the web or in print," he wrote earlier this year. A pathologist who has long been on the faculty of the University of Michigan Medical School, Friedman elaborated on his comment in a telephone conversation with me. His thinking, he said, has taken on a "staccato" quality, reflecting the way he quickly scans short passages of text from many sources online. "I can't read *War and Peace* anymore," he admitted. "I've lost the ability to do that. Even a blog post of more than three or four paragraphs is too much to absorb. I skim it."

Anecdotes alone don't prove much. And we still await the long-term neurological and psychological experiments that will provide a definitive picture of how Internet use affects cognition. But a recently published study of online research habits , conducted by scholars from University College London, suggests that we may well be in the midst of a sea change in the way we read and think. As part of the five-year research program, the scholars examined computer logs documenting the behavior of visitors to two popular research sites, one operated by the British Library and one by a U.K. educational consortium, that provide access to journal articles, e-books, and other sources of written information. They found that people using the sites exhibited "a form of skimming activity," hopping from one source to another and rarely returning to any source they'd already visited. They typically read no more than one or two pages of an article or book before they would "bounce" out to another site. Sometimes they'd save a long article, but there's no evidence that they ever went back and actually read it. The authors of the study report:

> It is clear that users are not reading online in the traditional sense; indeed there are signs that new forms of "reading" are emerging as users "power browse" horizontally through titles, contents pages and abstracts going for quick wins. It almost seems that they go online to avoid reading in the traditional sense.

Thanks to the ubiquity of text on the Internet, not to mention the popularity of text-messaging on cell phones, we may well be reading more today than we did in the 1970s or 1980s, when television was our medium of choice. But it's a different kind of reading, and behind it lies a different kind of thinking—perhaps even a new sense of the self. "We are not only what we read," says Maryanne Wolf, a developmental psychologist at Tufts University and the author of *Proust and the Squid: The Story and Science of the Reading Brain*. "We are *how* we read." Wolf worries that the style of reading promoted by the Net, a style that puts "efficiency" and "immediacy" above all else, may be weakening our capacity for the kind of deep reading that emerged when an earlier technology, the printing press, made long and complex works of prose commonplace. When we read online, she says, we tend to become "mere decoders of information." Our ability to interpret text, to make the rich mental connections that form when we read deeply and without distraction, remains largely disengaged.

Reading, explains Wolf, is not an instinctive skill for human beings. It's not etched into our genes the way speech is. We have to teach our minds how to translate the symbolic characters we see into the language we understand. And the media or other technologies we use in learning and practicing the craft of reading play an important part in shaping the neural circuits inside our brains. Experiments demonstrate that readers of ideograms, such as the Chinese, develop a mental circuitry for reading that is very different from the circuitry found in those of us whose written language employs an alphabet. The variations extend across many regions of the brain, including those that govern such essential cognitive functions as memory and the interpretation of visual and auditory stimuli. We can expect as well that the circuits woven by our use of the Net will be different from those woven by our reading of books and other printed works.

Sometime in 1882, Friedrich Nietzsche bought a typewriter—a Malling-Hansen Writing Ball, to be precise. His vision was failing, and keeping his eyes focused on a page had become exhausting and painful, often bringing on crushing headaches. He had been forced to curtail his writing, and he feared that he would soon have to give it up. The typewriter rescued him, at least for a time. Once he had mastered touch-typing, he was able to write with his eyes closed, using only the tips of his fingers. Words could once again flow from his mind to the page.

But the machine had a subtler effect on his work. One of Nietzsche's friends, a composer, noticed a change in the style of his writing. His already terse prose had become even tighter, more telegraphic. "Perhaps you will through this instrument even take to a new idiom," the friend wrote in a letter, noting that, in his own work, his "'thoughts' in music and language often depend on the quality of pen and paper."

"You are right," Nietzsche replied, "our writing equipment takes part in the forming of our thoughts." Under the sway of the machine, writes the German media scholar Friedrich A. Kittler , Nietzsche's prose "changed from arguments to aphorisms, from thoughts to puns, from rhetoric to telegram style."

The human brain is almost infinitely malleable. People used to think that our mental meshwork, the dense connections formed among the 100 billion or so neurons inside our skulls, was largely fixed by the time we reached adulthood. But brain researchers have discovered that that's not the case. James Olds, a professor of neuroscience who directs the Krasnow Institute for Advanced Study at George Mason University, says that even the adult mind "is very plastic." Nerve cells routinely break old connections and form new ones. "The brain," according to Olds, "has the ability to reprogram itself on the fly, altering the way it functions."

As we use what the sociologist Daniel Bell has called our "intellectual technologies"—the tools that extend our mental rather than our physical capacities—we inevitably begin to take on the qualities of those technologies. The mechanical clock, which came into common use in the 14th century, provides a compelling example. In *Technics and Civilization*, the historian and cultural critic Lewis Mumford described how the clock "disassociated time from human events and helped create the belief in an independent world of mathematically measurable sequences." The "abstract framework of divided time" became "the point of reference for both action and thought."

The clock's methodical ticking helped bring into being the scientific mind and the scientific man. But it also took something away. As the late MIT computer scientist Joseph Weizenbaum observed in his 1976 book, *Computer Power and Human Reason: From Judgment to Calculation*, the conception of the world that emerged from the widespread use of timekeeping instruments "remains an impoverished version of the older one, for it rests on a rejection of those direct experiences that formed the basis for, and indeed constituted, the old reality." In deciding when to eat, to work, to sleep, to rise, we stopped listening to our senses and started obeying the clock.

The process of adapting to new intellectual technologies is reflected in the changing metaphors we use to explain ourselves to ourselves. When the mechanical clock arrived, people began thinking of their brains as operating "like clockwork." Today, in the age of software, we have come to think of them as operating "like computers." But the changes, neuroscience tells us, go much deeper than metaphor. Thanks to our brain's plasticity, the adaptation occurs also at a biological level.

The Internet promises to have particularly far-reaching effects on cognition. In a paper published in 1936, the British mathematician Alan Turing proved that a digital computer, which at the time existed only as a theoretical machine, could be programmed to perform the function of any other information-processing device. And that's what we're seeing today. The Internet, an immeasurably powerful computing system, is subsuming most of our other intellectual technologies. It's becoming our map and our clock, our printing press and our typewriter, our calculator and our telephone, and our radio and TV.

When the Net absorbs a medium, that medium is re-created in the Net's image. It injects the medium's content with hyperlinks, blinking ads, and other digital gewgaws, and it surrounds the content with the content of all the other media it has absorbed. A new e-mail message, for instance, may announce its arrival as we're glancing over the latest headlines at a newspaper's site. The result is to scatter our attention and diffuse our concentration.

The Net's influence doesn't end at the edges of a computer screen, either. As people's minds become attuned to the crazy quilt of Internet media, traditional media have to adapt to the audience's new expectations. Television programs add text crawls and pop-up ads, and magazines and newspapers shorten their articles, introduce capsule summaries, and crowd their pages with easy-to-browse info-snippets. When, in March of this year, *The New York Times* decided to devote the second and third pages of every edition to article abstracts , its design director, Tom Bodkin, explained that the "shortcuts" would give harried readers a quick "taste" of the day's news, sparing them the "less efficient" method of actually turning the pages and reading the articles. Old media have little choice but to play by the new-media rules.

Never has a communications system played so many roles in our lives—or exerted such broad influence over our thoughts—as the Internet does today. Yet, for all that's been written about the Net, there's been little consideration of how, exactly, it's reprogramming us. The Net's intellectual ethic remains obscure.

About the same time that Nietzsche started using his typewriter, an earnest young man named Frederick Winslow Taylor carried a stopwatch into the Midvale Steel plant in Philadelphia and began a historic series of experiments aimed at improving the efficiency of the plant's machinists. With the approval of Midvale's owners, he recruited a group of factory hands, set them to work on various metalworking machines, and recorded and timed their every movement as well as the operations of the machines. By breaking down every job into a sequence of small, discrete steps and then testing different ways of performing each one, Taylor created a set of precise instructions—an "algorithm," we might say today—for how each worker should work. Midvale's employees grumbled about the strict new regime, claiming that it turned them into little more than automatons, but the factory's productivity soared.

More than a hundred years after the invention of the steam engine, the Industrial Revolution had at last found its philosophy and its philosopher.

Taylor's tight industrial choreography—his "system," as he liked to call it—was embraced by manufacturers throughout the country and, in time, around the world. Seeking maximum speed, maximum efficiency, and maximum output, factory owners used time-and-motion studies to organize their work and configure the jobs of their workers. The goal, as Taylor defined it in his celebrated 1911 treatise, *The Principles of Scientific Management*, was to identify and adopt, for every job, the "one best method" of work and thereby to effect "the gradual substitution of science for rule of thumb throughout the mechanic arts." Once his system was applied to all acts of manual labor, Taylor assured his followers, it would bring about a restructuring not only of industry but of society, creating a utopia of perfect efficiency. "In the past the man has been first," he declared; "in the future the system must be first."

Taylor's system is still very much with us; it remains the ethic of industrial manufacturing. And now, thanks to the growing power that computer engineers and software coders wield over our intellectual lives, Taylor's ethic is beginning to govern the realm of the mind as well. The Internet is a machine designed for the efficient and automated collection, transmission, and manipulation of information, and its legions of programmers are intent on finding the "one best method"—the perfect algorithm—to carry out every mental movement of what we've come to describe as "knowledge work."

Google's headquarters, in Mountain View, California—the Googleplex—is the Internet's high church, and the religion practiced inside its walls is Taylorism. Google, says its chief executive, Eric Schmidt, is "a company that's founded around the science of measurement," and it is striving to "systematize everything" it does. Drawing on the terabytes of behavioral data it collects through its search engine and other sites, it carries out thousands of experiments a day, according to the *Harvard Business Review*, and it uses the results to refine the algorithms that increasingly control how people find information and extract meaning from it. What Taylor did for the work of the hand, Google is doing for the work of the mind.

The company has declared that its mission is "to organize the world's information and make it universally accessible and useful." It seeks to develop "the perfect search engine," which it defines as something that "understands exactly what you mean and gives you back exactly what you want." In Google's view, information is a kind of commodity, a utilitarian resource that can be mined and processed with industrial efficiency. The more pieces of information we can "access" and the faster we can extract their gist, the more productive we become as thinkers.

Where does it end? Sergey Brin and Larry Page, the gifted young men who founded Google while pursuing doctoral degrees in computer science at Stanford, speak frequently of their desire to turn their search engine into an artificial intelligence, a HAL-like machine that might be connected directly to our brains. "The ultimate search engine is something as smart as people—or smarter," Page said in a speech a few years back. "For us, working on search is a way to work on artificial intelligence." In a 2004 interview with *Newsweek*, Brin said, "Certainly if you had all the world's information directly attached to your brain, or an artificial brain that was smarter than your brain, you'd be better off." Last year, Page told a convention of scientists that Google is "really trying to build artificial intelligence and to do it on a large scale."

Such an ambition is a natural one, even an admirable one, for a pair of math whizzes with vast quantities of cash at their disposal and a small army of computer scientists in their employ. A fundamentally scientific enterprise, Google is motivated by a desire to use technology, in Eric Schmidt's words, "to solve problems that have never been solved before," and artificial intelligence is the hardest problem out there. Why wouldn't Brin and Page want to be the ones to crack it?

Still, their easy assumption that we'd all "be better off" if our brains were supplemented, or even replaced, by an artificial intelligence is unsettling. It suggests a belief that intelligence is the output of a mechanical process, a series of discrete steps that can be isolated, measured, and optimized. In Google's world, the world we enter when we go online, there's little place for the fuzziness of contemplation. Ambiguity is not an opening for insight but a bug to be fixed. The human brain is just an outdated computer that needs a faster processor and a bigger hard drive.

The idea that our minds should operate as high-speed data-processing machines is not only built into the workings of the Internet, it is the network's reigning business model as well. The faster we surf across the Web—the more links we click and pages we view—the more opportunities Google and other companies gain to collect information about us and to feed us advertisements. Most of the proprietors of the commercial Internet have a financial stake in collecting the crumbs of data we leave behind as we flit from link to link—the more crumbs, the better. The last thing these companies want is to encourage leisurely reading or slow, concentrated thought. It's in their economic interest to drive us to distraction.

Maybe I'm just a worrywart. Just as there's a tendency to glorify technological progress, there's a countertendency to expect the worst of every new tool or machine. In Plato's *Phaedrus*, Socrates bemoaned the development of writing. He feared that, as people came to rely on the written word as a substitute for the knowledge they used to carry inside their heads, they would, in the words of one of the dialogue's characters, "cease to exercise their memory and become forgetful." And because they would be able to "receive a quantity of information without proper instruction," they would "be thought very knowledgeable when they are for the most part quite ignorant." They would be "filled with the conceit of wisdom instead of real wisdom." Socrates wasn't wrong—the new technology did often have the effects he feared—but he was shortsighted. He couldn't foresee the many ways that writing and reading would serve to spread information, spur fresh ideas, and expand human knowledge (if not wisdom).

The arrival of Gutenberg's printing press, in the 15th century, set off another round of teeth gnashing. The Italian humanist Hieronimo Squarciafico worried that the easy availability of books would lead to intellectual laziness, making men "less studious" and weakening their minds. Others argued that cheaply printed books and broadsheets would undermine religious authority, demean the work of scholars and scribes, and spread sedition and debauchery. As New York University professor Clay Shirky notes, "Most of the arguments made against the printing press were correct, even prescient." But, again, the doomsayers were unable to imagine the myriad blessings that the printed word would deliver.

So, yes, you should be skeptical of my skepticism. Perhaps those who dismiss critics of the Internet as Luddites or nostalgists will be proved correct, and from our hyperactive, data-stoked minds will spring a golden age of intellectual discovery and universal wisdom. Then again, the Net isn't the alphabet, and although it may replace the printing press, it produces something altogether different. The kind of deep reading that a sequence of printed pages promotes is valuable not just for the knowledge we acquire from the author's words but for the intellectual vibrations those words set off within our own minds. In the quiet spaces opened up by the sustained, undistracted reading of a book, or by any other act of contemplation, for that matter, we make our own associations, draw our own inferences and analogies, foster our own ideas. Deep reading, as Maryanne Wolf argues, is indistinguishable from deep thinking.

If we lose those quiet spaces, or fill them up with "content," we will sacrifice something important not only in our selves but in our culture. In a recent essay, the playwright Richard Foreman eloquently described what's at stake:

> I come from a tradition of Western culture, in which the ideal (my ideal) was the complex, dense and "cathedral-like" structure of the highly educated and articulate personality—a man or woman who carried inside themselves a personally constructed and unique version of the entire heritage of the West. [But now] I see within us all (myself included) the replacement of complex inner density with a new kind of self—evolving under the pressure of information overload and the technology of the "instantly available."

As we are drained of our "inner repertory of dense cultural inheritance," Foreman concluded, we risk turning into "'pancake people'—spread wide and thin as we connect with that vast network of information accessed by the mere touch of a button."

I'm haunted by that scene in *2001*. What makes it so poignant, and so weird, is the computer's emotional response to the disassembly of its mind: its despair as one circuit after another goes dark, its childlike pleading with the astronaut—"I can feel it. I can feel it. I'm afraid"—and its final reversion to what can only be called a state of innocence. HAL's outpouring of feeling contrasts with the emotionlessness that characterizes the human figures in the film, who go about their business with an almost robotic efficiency. Their thoughts and actions feel scripted, as if they're following the steps of an algorithm. In the world of *2001*, people have become so machinelike that the most human character turns out to be a machine. That's the essence of Kubrick's dark prophecy: as we come to rely on computers to mediate our understanding of the world, it is our own intelligence that flattens into artificial intelligence.

## Content

1. How does Carr characterize "deep reading" versus reading on-line?
2. What evidence does Carr use to prove that technology changes the human brain?
3. According to Carr, why is the commodification of information a problem?

## Craft

1. Why does Carr introduce and conclude his essay with scenes from Kubric's *2001: A Space Odyssey*? How effective are references to films given the chances readers may or may not have seen the movie?

2. Carr acknowledges that "as there's a tendency to glorify technological progress, there's a countertendency to expect the worst of every new tool or machine." By doing so he introduces counter-claims or reasons why people might disagree with his argument. Does doing so strengthen or weaken the essay? Explain your answer.

3. The article's title "Is Google Making Us Stupid" is followed by the subtitle "What the Internet is doing to our brains." Which title most accurately reflects the content of Carr's essay? Why might an author or editor choose one title over the other?

4. Does Carr's essay use a specific pattern of organization? How does this pattern (or lack of a pattern) help readers understand his message?

## Contemplation

1. Compile a list of ways technology shapes your daily experience. After reviewing your list, do you agree with Carr's claim that the internet is changing the way we read, live, and think? Are these changes positive or negative? How can people take the best of what the internet has to offer while minimalizing the harmful effects?

### Assignment

#### Take the No Technology Challenge

Challenge yourself to spend a single day without using your phone, computer, or television. You may choose to give up one device or all devices. If you have responsibilities that you cannot ignore, you may strike a balance by putting your phone on silent and only taking the call if it's required for work or family. Plan ahead so you can comfortably set aside a day without missing any deadlines or worrying about an upcoming homework assignment.

When the day is over, write a one page essay reflecting on your experience.

Your essay might consider the following questions:

When were you most tempted to turn on your device? Did you give in to the impulse? What alternatives did you find for Googling information or texting a friend? How did you spend your time? How did your interactions and daily habits change? How did going without technology make you feel and why? Would you recommend the no-technology challenge to a friend?

# Is Fiction Good For Us?

## by Jonathan Gottschall

*Jonathan Gottschall, who teaches at Washington and Jefferson College, writes at the intersection of literature and science. His first book,* The Rape of Troy: Evolution, Violence, and the World of Homer, *examines ancient Greek epic poetry from the perspective of evolutionary psychology.* The Storytelling Animal, *named as an editor's choice by* The New York Times, *uses science, psychology, and history to explore the role of fiction in human society. In this essay, Gottschall summarizes some of his research from* The Storytelling Animal *and* Graphing Jane Austen. *Along the way, he asks the fundamental questions: why do people love stories and how do stories shape our lives?*

Is fiction good for us? We spend huge chunks of our lives immersed in novels, films, TV shows and other forms of fiction. Some see this as a positive thing, arguing that made-up stories cultivate our mental and moral development. But others have argued that fiction is mentally and ethically corrosive. It's an ancient question: Does fiction build the morality of individuals and societies, or does it break it down?

This controversy has been flaring up—sometimes literally, in the form of book burnings—ever since Plato tried to ban fiction from his ideal republic. In 1961, Federal Communications Commission Chairman Newton Minow famously said that television was not working in "the public interest" because its "formula comedies about totally unbelievable families, blood and thunder, mayhem, violence, sadism, murder, Western bad men, Western good men, private eyes, gangsters, more violence and cartoons" amounted to a "vast wasteland." And what he said of TV programming has also been said, over the centuries, of novels, theater, comic books and films: They are not in the public interest.

Until recently, we've only been able to guess about the actual psychological effects of fiction on individuals and society. But new research in psychology and broad-based literary analysis is finally taking questions about morality out of the realm of speculation.

This research consistently shows that fiction does mold us. The more deeply we are cast under a story's spell, the more potent its influence. In fact, fiction seems to be more effective at changing beliefs than nonfiction, which is designed to persuade through argument and evidence. Studies show that when we read nonfiction, we read with our shields up. We are critical and

Gottschall, Jonathan. "Is Fiction Good For Us?" *Boston Globe.* Boston Globe Media Partners, 29 April 2010. Web. 27 May 2016. Carr, Nicholas. Rpt. in *Decorum.* Ed. Kristina Gladfelter and Melody Niesen. Revised 2nd ed. Southlake, TX: Fountainhead, 2016. 159-164. Print.

skeptical. But when we are absorbed in a story, we drop our intellectual guard. We are moved emotionally, and this seems to make us rubbery and easy to shape.

But perhaps the most impressive finding is just how fiction shapes us: mainly for the better, not for the worse. Fiction enhances our ability to understand other people; it promotes a deep morality that cuts across religious and political creeds. More peculiarly, fiction's happy endings seem to warp our sense of reality. They make us believe in a lie: that the world is more just than it actually is. But believing that lie has important effects for society—and it may even help explain why humans tell stories in the first place.

It's not that hard to see why social critics have often been dismayed by fiction. We spend a huge amount of time lost in stories, with the average American spending four hours per day watching television.

And if the sheer time investment were not enough, there's the content. Since fiction's earliest beginnings, morally repulsive behavior has been a great staple of the stories we tell. From the sickening sexual violence of *The Girl With the Dragon Tattoo* to the deranged sadism of Shakespeare's Titus Andronicus, to Oedipus stabbing his eyes out in disgust, to the horrors portrayed on TV shows like *Breaking Bad* and *CSI*—throughout time, the most popular stories have often featured the most unpleasant subject matter. Fiction's obsession with filth and vice has led critics of different stripes to condemn plays, novels, comic books and TV for corroding values and corrupting youth.

Moreover, it's clear that these stories really can change our views. As psychologist Raymond Mar writes, "Researchers have repeatedly found that reader attitudes shift to become more congruent with the ideas expressed in a [fictional] narrative." For example, studies reliably show that when we watch a TV show that treats gay families nonjudgmentally (say, *Modern Family*), our own views on homosexuality are likely to move in the same nonjudgmental direction. History, too, reveals fiction's ability to change our values at the societal level, for better and worse. For example, Harriet Beecher Stowe's *Uncle Tom's Cabin* helped bring about the Civil War by convincing huge numbers of Americans that blacks are people and that enslaving them is a mortal sin. On the other hand, the 1915 film *The Birth of a Nation* inflamed racist sentiments and helped resurrect an all but defunct Ku Klux Klan.

So those who are concerned about the messages in fiction, whether they are conservative or liberal, have a point. Fiction is dangerous because it has the power to modify the principles of individuals and whole societies.

But fiction is doing something that all political factions should be able to get behind. Beyond the local battles of the culture wars, virtually all storytelling, regardless of genre, increases society's fund of empathy and reinforces an ethic of decency that is deeper than politics.

For a long time, literary critics and philosophers, along with the novelist George Eliot, have argued that one of fiction's main jobs is to "enlarge men's sympathies." Recent lab work suggests they are right. The psychologists Mar and Keith Oatley tested the idea that entering fiction's simulated social worlds enhances our ability to connect with actual human beings. They found that heavy fiction readers outperformed heavy nonfiction readers on tests of empathy, even after they controlled for the possibility that people who already had high empathy might naturally gravitate to fiction. As Oatley puts it, fiction serves the function of "making the world a better place by improving interpersonal understanding."

Follow-up studies have reached similar conclusions. For example, one study showed that 4- to 6-year-old children who were exposed to a large number of children's books and films had a significantly stronger ability to read the mental and emotional states of other people.

Similarly, Washington & Lee psychologist Dan Johnson recently had people read a short story that was specifically written to induce compassion in the reader. He wanted to see not only if fiction increased empathy, but whether it would lead to actual helping behavior. Johnson found that the more absorbed subjects were in the story, the more empathy they felt, and the more empathy they felt, the more likely the subjects were to help when the experimenter "accidentally" dropped a handful of pens—highly absorbed readers were twice as likely to help out.

"In conclusion," Johnson writes, "it appears that curling up with a good book may do more than provide relaxation and entertainment. Reading narrative fiction allows one to learn about our social world and as a result fosters empathic growth and pro-social behavior."

Similarly, novelists such as Leo Tolstoy and John Gardner have contended that fiction is morally beneficial, and here, too, research is bearing them out. While fiction often dwells on lewdness, depravity and simple selfishness, storytellers virtually always put us in a position to judge wrongdoing, and we do so with gusto.

As the Brandeis literary scholar William Flesch argues, fiction all over the world is strongly dominated by the theme of poetic justice. Generally speaking, goodness is endorsed and rewarded, and badness is condemned and punished. Stories, from modern films to ancient fairy tales, steep us all in the same powerful norms and values. True, antiheroes, from Milton's Satan to Tony Soprano, captivate us, but bad guys are almost never allowed to live happily ever after. And fiction generally teaches us that it is profitable to be good.

Take a study of television viewers by the Austrian psychologist Marcus Appel. Appel points out that for a society to function properly, people have to believe in justice. They have to believe that there are rewards for doing right and punishments for doing wrong. And, indeed, people generally do believe that life punishes the vicious and rewards the virtuous. But one class of people appears to believe these things in particular: those who consume a lot of fiction.

In Appel's study, people who mainly watched drama and comedy on TV— as opposed to heavy viewers of news programs and documentaries—had substantially stronger "just-world" beliefs. Appel concludes that fiction, by constantly exposing us to the theme of poetic justice, may be partly responsible for the sense that the world is, on the whole, a just place.

This is despite the fact, as Appel puts it, "that this is patently not the case." As people who watch the news know very well, bad things happen to good people all the time, and most crimes go unpunished. In other words, fiction seems to teach us to see the world through rose-colored lenses. And the fact that we see the world that way seems to be an important part of what makes human societies work.

All these questions about the effects of fiction lead up to one big one: Why are humans storytelling animals at all? Why are we, as a species, so hopelessly addicted to narratives about the fake struggles of pretend people? Evolution is a ruthlessly utilitarian process. How has the seeming luxury of fiction—the apparent waste in time and creative energy—not been eliminated by the evolutionary process?

One possibility is that fiction has hidden benefits that outweigh its costs. For instance, anthropologists have long argued that stories have group-level benefits. Traditional tales, from hero epics to sacred myths, perform the essential work of defining group identity and reinforcing cultural values.

Along with three colleagues, the literary scholar Joseph Carroll and the psychologists John Johnson and Dan Kruger, I wanted to explore the possibility that fiction generally—not just folk tales—may act as a kind of social glue among humans, binding fractious individuals together around common values. So we asked hundreds of literary scholars and avid readers to respond to a questionnaire about 19th-century British novels.

We asked them to answer questions about the motives and personalities of characters, and to classify them as protagonists or antagonists; we also asked questions that explored how readers felt about these characters. The results showed that antagonists and protagonists had sharply differentiated personalities. Antagonists were overwhelmingly driven by motives of power, wealth and prestige. They didn't care about winning mates, making friends or even helping their own kin. They were loveless, emotionally isolated egomaniacs. The protagonists, meanwhile, were keen on romance and eager to help their friends and relatives.

These results, which will be published in a book called *Graphing Jane Austen*, may seem unsurprising: In short, our heroes are heroes. But our findings were consistent with the work of anthropologist Chris Boehm, who studies social dynamics in hunter-gatherers. Boehm notes that hunter-gatherers are egalitarian, with all members of the tribe coming together to suppress bully-boy behavior in individuals. The same kind of dynamic applies in the simulated social worlds of Victorian novels. The bad guys in these ultra-"civilized" Victorian novels were like the bullies in a hunter-gatherer band, while the good guys were self-effacing and cooperative.

Our survey respondents reacted to the characters as though they were real people: They admired the protagonists, disliked the antagonists, felt happy when the good guys succeeded and felt sad or angry when they were threatened. By simulating a world where anti-social behavior is strongly condemned and punished, these novels were promoting ancient human values. And from these books, and from fiction more broadly, readers learn by association that if they are more like the protagonists, they'll be more likely to live happily ever after.

Fiction is often treated like a mere frill in human life, if not something worse. But the emerging science of story suggests that fiction is good for more than kicks. By enhancing empathy, fiction reduces social friction. At the same time, story exerts a kind of magnetic force, drawing us together around common values. In other words, most fiction, even the trashy stuff, appears to be in the public interest after all.

# Content

1. How have commentators and thinkers conceptualized the impact of fiction in the past? How is technology changing the way researchers understand fiction?

2. According to Gottschall, how does fiction benefit society?

3. What are some of the proposed evolutionary advantages of humans being "wired for stories?"

4. According to Gottschall, how does fiction encourage the reader's view of a just world? How does this view differ from reality? Given the difference, is a fictional sense of justice helpful or harmful?

# Craft

1. What is Gottschall's thesis statement? Is his thesis clearly stated or implied?

2. What evidence does Gottschall provide to support his claim that stories positively change our views of people and society? Which of these examples did you find most compelling?

3. How does Gottschall use questions to engage readers?

# Contemplation

1. Gottschall spends the latter portion of his essay discussing viewers' responses to heroes and villains. He states, "Our survey respondents reacted to the characters as though they were real people: They admired the protagonists, disliked the antagonists, felt happy when the good guys succeeded and felt sad or angry when they were threatened." When you reflect on your favorite fictional characters, do you gravitate more toward heroes or villains? Why do these characters appeal to you? How does your response compare to the responses in Gottschall's survey?

## Assignment

### Write a Persuasive Analysis

Fictional stories and the characters that inhabit them have a tremendous influence over our lives and our culture. For example, most of what you know about pirates does not come from the pages of history; rather it comes from the pages of *Treasure Island* by Robert Lewis Stevenson. Similarly most of us have never visited Paris, but we have an idea of what it is like from the stories and films we have encountered. As a result, fiction can open up world and lives we otherwise never would have encountered. At the same time, it can set the stage for stereotypes, misconceptions, and even anti-social behavior.

Write a **four-page (1000-word) persuasive analysis** of a character from a book, film, television series, or video game. You will persuade your readers that this character has **either** a positive or negative impact on society.

**Select one character from one specific medium**. [For example, if you choose Batman, specify you are analyzing Batman from *The Dark Knight Rises*. Different adaptations present very difference characters, so you want to focus on one specific incarnation of the character.] Secondly, **analyze the character's impact on one specific group of people**. [For example, you could look at the impact of a Disney princess on little girls or the impact of Ezio, from *Assassin's Creed*, on teenage boys. The media affects different audiences in different ways, so it is important to be specific about the audience you are discussing].

Finally, your persuasive claim should be based on a careful analysis of the character. For this assignment, you should analyze the character's actions, appearance, attitude, and speech. These details will reveal important messages and values that are subtly communicated to the audience. Your analysis will probably reveal more details than you can fit in a four-page essay. Therefore, when you write, you should select details that directly support your thesis statement. In addition, your essay should contain the following:

- A thesis statement that makes a claim about the impact of the character on one specific audience
- An analysis of the character that reveals the values, stereotypes, or messages the character represents
- A discussion of the positive or negative impact on the audience
- Provide context (When, where, and for whom was this character created)

Some things you should consider doing to help support your thesis:
- Think about what values, stereotypes, or messages the character embodies. How are these messages shown in the way the character looks, acts, and speaks?
- Examine the character's actions and attitudes. Then explain how they impact the audience.
- Consider representation (Does this character accurately represent the real world or does it send a distorted message about the world?)
- Is this character complex or stereotypical?
- Consider the role of the media in people's lives.

The following essays, submitted by UCM students, provide examples of the three types of writing commonly assigned in college: expressive, informative, and persuasive. The final essay compares a student's rough and final draft. These two versions are printed on facing pages so you can follow along with the student's revisions.

Jacob Kaufman
Joseph Alfino
ENGL 2010
Date Month Year

### Night Flight

Pappy Boyington, a World War II pilot and Medal of Honor recipient once said, "Flying is hours and hours of boredom sprinkled with a few seconds of sheer terror." In most situations, the boredom goes unnoticed, attributed to being just another flight. However, one flight never leaves a young pilot's mind: flying at night. The sweet sailing under the quiet hum of metal sails is awe-inspiring, which gives a sense of peace and serenity between the "few seconds of sheer terror."

The airfield at night is an intimidating place. Very few fly at night, and even then out of necessity, and not the pleasure of doing so. The ramp is dark, the airplanes cold, and the tarmac unforgiving. The frailty of one small light helps a single pilot carry out his preflight inspection. The sleeping aircraft is poked and prodded, and once the pilot is happy, he climbs in, ready to stir it to life. An aircraft engine pierces the cold, dark air as it is fired up. It's the only sound aside from the occasional cricket or rustle in the grass. Inside the cockpit, only a few tiny lights show that the metal bird is still alive and well, and the muffled purr of the engine through a thick headset confirms this. A few final checks are made, and the brakes are released.

The engine noise rises as the gauges twitch and the pilot steers his plane towards the runway, a single floodlight coming from the wing and showing the way. He reaches the end of the runway and looks out with only a few lights to be seen marking the runway. An old rule of flying runs through the pilot's head: every takeoff is optional, but every landing is mandatory. Final checks are run, and the bird strains against the brakes to fly into the air, its engine revving to hurdle the pilot and plane into the inky blankness of the sky. The brakes are released, and lights start zipping by. Focus is concentrated on staying straight on the ground, following a single dashed line as the plane bumps over small cracks. Finally, the speed grows enough and the pilot pulls back, sending him and his craft into the wild black wonder of sky.

Then, nothing. Nothing but the hum of the engine, and the gauges in front of the lone pilot. Only a small light keeps the pilot aware that the plane is even flying, the gauges it illuminates providing a wealth of information to the trained eye. In the smooth, soft air, pinpricks of light start to dot the sky. More and more appear, more than a normal person can see from their bedroom window. The single light inside is turned down, and a tapestry splattered with brilliant whites and yellows unveils in front of the pilot's eyes. The pilot levels off and pulls back the throttle in order to not tire the bird too quickly, and the roar dulls to a hum. Towns and streets and roads can be seen below, with headlights darting back and forth, to and fro. The lights wind out like spider's legs from every road, curving and diving as they are shown only for brief moments in a car travelling along it. Flying so slowly, it's like being suspended in space, enveloped by a cool, black sheet filled with holes. The air is so smooth, it's as if the plane wasn't even there, and the pilot had sat on a magic carpet, able to fly anywhere and see anything. The seconds become minutes, and the minutes become an hour.

The soft voice of an air traffic controller breaks the pilot's slight reverie of watching the lights sail by below. It startles the pilot, but is welcome. Like an old friend, she speaks in code to the pilot, guiding him to the safe haven of the airport he was bound towards. The smiles could almost be felt through the voices as they thank each other, the pilot returning to his plane and the controller to her coffee. To the pilot's trained eye a dark hole in the lights becomes an airport, and he focuses himself away from the beauty around him to his task at hand - landing safely.

Anyone else's natural instincts would think it is crazy to land an airplane at night. The pilot knows better. Patterns of red, green and white show him exactly where to go, and how to fly. Inside his chest a tightness from instinct is there, as he is unable to see the runway itself. The comforting hum of the engine is nonexistent, the power pulled back to let the craft glide on its own momentum. The tradeoff between altitude and distance is a tricky one, especially at night, and does not serve as comfort to the pilot if the lights are displaced even the slightest bit. Finally, a single beam of light from the plane illuminates the black concrete below. Electric motors whirr as the flaps are pushed into the wind, jolting the pilot forward and slowing the craft down. A few moments later, the pilot pulls back, and the plane kisses the runway with a delightful chirp. The worst is over, and the pilot turns off the runway, consciously reminding himself to breathe. He pulls into his parking space, and shuts down the bird, putting it to sleep until the next pilot comes around.

Even though flying is hours and hours of boredom sprinkled with a few seconds of sheer terror, boredom is circumstantial. Many pilots would call a night flight boring. However, to anyone who has had the chance to fly at night with only themselves and their airplane, it can be a surreal experience, punctuated at the ends with a few seconds of sheer terror.

John Hagan
Melody Niesen
Composition 1020
November 16, 2014

Breeding the Perfect Human

Doctors are constantly attempting to create more effective forms of medication in order to better the lives of human beings through medical advancements. However, these medical achievements often bring up ethical problems. This predicament is an extremely pressing issue for which the government has yet to achieve an acceptable response. New issues arise nearly every day; the legal responses tend to be controversial and seldom appease both parties. These issues leave unanswered questions and create morally grey areas that tend to become, at the very least, messy. Due to non-specific laws, often times injustices occur causing people lifetimes of difficulty and detriment to a large portion of the population's personal health.

Rebecca Skloot's 2010 best-selling novel, *The Immortal Life of Henrietta Lacks*, es an extremely controversial medical case. The story takes place in the early 1950s and gives an in-depth recollection of the injustices that occurred to a middle aged black woman named Henrietta Lacks. Shortly before dying of cervical cancer, Lacks signed a contract that gave consent to treat her illness. However, the doctors of The John Hopkins Hospital participated in experimental research that exceeded the medical contract of consent signed by Lacks. In spite of this ethical issue, the research was extremely successful and ended up contributing to numerous medical advancements. Regardless of the success, neither the Lacks family nor her family ever received any form of compensation from the advancement despite her cells, and research based off of her cells, being worth large amounts of money.

Although it has been a substantial amount of time since this ethical controversy occurred, the problem of morality in the medical field is still very much alive in modern times. On November 16, 2014, in an article entitled "Combining The DNA Of Three People Raises Ethical Questions," Rob Stein explores a recent medical controversy involving the replacement of mitochondrial DNA in order to prevent birth defects in children. This article appears in an online news channel named *Shots* that strives to bring accurate unbiased modern medical issues to the eyes of the public. This research, while ground-breaking, is also heavily debated.

This DNA combination procedure is truly groundbreaking. A patient participating in this operation is ensuring that his or her child would potentially live a healthy life and not be held back by any possible genetic birth defects. This provides the ability to solve the medical issue before it even begins. The operation does not change the identity of the person; it simply takes away medical problems. The child is still fully the offspring of the mother and father. If humanity has the ability to end these genetic birth defects before they begin, it could contribute to a person's overall health and provide a longer lifespan.

Knowing the medical facts is extremely important in creating an opinion. In the article, "Combining The DNA Of Three People Raises Ethical Questions," women are willing to have this operation. In a lab north of England, "a team of scientists trying to replace defective DNA with healthy DNA. They hope this procedure could one day help women who are carrying genetic disorders have healthy children" (Stein). This means that scientists are attempting to erase the genetic problems that some families have dealt with for generations by replacing the mother's egg's DNA with a third parties' healthy cells. This article raises some of the same medical issues that Henrietta Lacks's situation does including informed consent, human research, and medicine in the legal field.

DNA combination is no small operation, "the researchers fertilize the egg, creating a very early embryo. Then they carefully remove all oft he DNA in the nucleus, leaving behind only the healthy mitochondrial DNA" (Stein). This essentially means that the baby will be the mother's child, but probable health defects could be erased leaving less chance for an unhealthy child. This could cure various medical problems and could be extremely beneficial to a human's life.

One major point Stein highlights for the process to be legalized is the case of Victoria Collins. The author explains that, "she [Collins] comes from a family that has had trouble having healthy babies for generations" (Stein). These complications could be fixed through the operation that these scientists are encouraging. Collins would be able to have healthy children and not need to be concerned that any of her genes would create problems with her child. However, when having a child that could possibly have three different types of DNA, one must have many concerns that complications may occur.

As of November of 2014, the process has not been legalized. Opponents of the operations proclaim that this is a masked form of eugenics. People are concerned that this may lead to the ability "to purchase for their children sort of genetic enhancements of certain characteristics like athletic ability or intelligence," (Stein). The results of this operation are unknown for humans because of the lack of research. This is only because the legal system has not been on board to this point. The operation has not been completed because, "The British scientists are waiting for government approval for the next step — transferring an embryo made this way into the womb of a woman trying to have a healthy baby" (Stein). This would make it possible to see what this operation could do for the medical world.

One medical issue that both pieces of literature explore is that of informed consent. Henrietta Lacks's fledgling education forced her to sign a document that she did not fully understand. She was desperate and should not have been coerced into making such a large decision. The combination of DNA presents a different problem with informed consent. The person that this operation would actually affect would be the child whose DNA was tampered with, but this person does not even exist yet! For obvious reasons, it would be impossible for the human that this operation actually effects to give informed consent. However, even when a child has been born, the medical decisions are still left in the parent's hands. The parent does not need to consult the child in regards to any medical issues when he or she is alive, so what is the difference? The parent that is deemed the primary caregiver should be able to make any decisions that will benefit the health and safety of the child (or future child).

This article and *The Immortal Life of Henrietta Lacks* communicate the same medical ethics issues through the morally gray area of human research. Doctors that participate in the combination of DNA do not know the long-term physical effects that this operation will have on the participant. They have not been able to test on humans because of research laws. The doctors that worked on Henrietta did not understand the long-term psychological effects that their research would have on the family. The research sparks an unwanted interest in the Lack's descendants. This family is essentially tortured mentally due to the research conducted on their ancestor.

The conclusion of the article explains that the future legalization for this operation is beginning to look bright. Dr. Sally Davies, "dismisses the worries about designer babies and children with three genetic parent." She continues to state, "The child will have the characteristics any other child would have in that family: intelligence, looks, behaviors, whatever. The only thing different would be those 37 genes in each mitochondria" (Stein). Davies is pushing to end genetic birth defects in children through the operation of combining DNA.

It is easy to be skeptical about these types of research. However, it is essential to look at the possibilities that these medical advances could have. The potential for this operation could be endless. This generation has the possibility to change the medical world. Medical consent and human research should not be overlooked, but as the article "Combining The DNA Of Three People Raises Ethical Questions" explains, this operation's benefits should not be overlooked. If the medical field can make advances such as the ones shown through *The Immortal Life of Henrietta Lacks*, but in an ethically correct manner, the human race could be changed forever.

Works Cited

"Combining The DNA Of Three People Raises Ethical Questions." *NPR*. NPR. Nov. 10 2014. Web. 17 Nov. 2014.

Skloot, Rebecca. *The Immortal Life of Henrietta Lacks*. New York: Crown, 2010. Print.

Maiesha Lane
Heather Hughes
Engl. 1020
18 November 2014

### Cinderella Said, So it is So

The smallest stroke of paint on an empty canvas, regardless of how many times it's covered up or repainted, will always be there. Though it may no longer be visible or relevant in what the canvas eventually becomes, it will still always be a part of that canvas. Children are much like empty canvases; when they are young, they do not have a perception of the world, or an idea of what it means to be beautiful or fortunate. They are utterly blank. It is what children are exposed to in their first few years in this world that becomes the small strokes of paint on the empty canvas that is their life. And unintentionally, as they mature, they begin to shape what they were first introduced to into their own ideas and views, thus providing the first strokes of paint. What they were initially exposed to is no longer relevant in their lives, but it shaped how they grew up, and what they believed in the process. The character Cinderella makes children believe in the notion that success derives from beauty, and that life itself revolves around the superficial aspects of wealth, power, and social status. She also teaches girls specifically that when they are faced with adverse situations, they should wait for a man to come and rescue them. This character paints a plethora of corrupted standards that will forever reside on the canvas that is the life of the child.

The character Cinderella derives from the beloved age-old Disney produced children's film *Cinderella*. In the movie, due to the death of her father, Cinderella is fated to live out her life under the supervision of her wicked stepmother who has two children of her own. With her father no longer around to ensure her well-being, Cinderella's stepmother and her jealous stepsisters, keep her enslaved and dress her in rags. Although Cinderella is oppressed, she possesses a trait that has potential to rescue her from her shockingly dreadful life; she is utterly beautiful. Consequently, she creates a standard of beauty in the minds of those who look up to her; typically young girls between the ages of four and ten. Cinderella inadvertently portrays the definition of beauty as being shorter, slender, having blue eyes, and having long blonde hair. Her step sisters, on the other hand, are portrayed as malevolent, and they both are completely unalike in appearance to Cinderella. They are both noticeably taller, they have black eyes, full hips, and hair that is a color other than blonde. One of them even has significantly shorter hair.

This makes children believe that whether they are beautiful or not comes down to how alike they look in comparison to Cinderella. In the film, Cinderella fell in love with the prince with the sole reason being physical attraction. Her stepsisters also displayed an interest in the prince, but they failed due to the fact that Cinderella was more attractive. This teaches children that in the event that they are pretty; everything works out in their favor.

When Cinderella was first introduced, she was indeed oppressed, but she was also more than capable of leaving her situation. However, she did not; she continued to live each day of her life succumbing to the tyranny of her step mother. Instead of Cinderella leaving her home on her own, and becoming her own savior, she waited for a man to come and set her free. In the movie, Cinderella was forbidden to attend the Royal Ball, until her fairy god mother appeared out of nowhere and magically made a beautiful dress and horse-drawn carriage appear. At the ball, Cinderella met the handsome, rich prince and in one dance, they fell in love. But Cinderella had to leave at midnight, because then, her dress and carriage would transform into the rags from which they originated. In the end, the prince found Cinderella by a shoe that she left behind in the midst of fleeing, and they marry, and live happily ever after. Cinderella knew the prince for roughly a day before he rode in on a white horse and asked for her hand in marriage, and she gladly accepted. So the reality of it is, Cinderella did not fall for the prince, she fell for the idea that she could trade in her situation for a better life and an extravagant castle and it would take no effort on her part. This makes young girls believe that when faced with adverse situations, they should wait for a man to come and rescue them.

When Cinderella became the prince's princess, all those who had been advocates for her failure had suddenly become her greatest admirers. Before Cinderella married the prince, she was worth little to nothing to her stepmother and her stepsisters. They were embarrassed to be seen with her outside of their home, and they couldn't have cared less as to whether she was properly fed and clothed. She was virtually their slave. But when Cinderella married into royalty, her stepmother and her step sister's attitudes toward her changed dramatically. They began to find it necessary to be in her good graces. Cinderella's step mother began to treat her like the daughter she always wanted, but never had. It's a simple lesson really; the rich are respected and the poor are ridiculed. This blatantly shows children that social status is everything when determining how to treat people.

In the words of Johnathan Gottschall, "The characters in fiction are just wiggles of ink on paper (or chemicals stains on celluloid). And yet ink people press effortlessly through the porous membrane separating their inky world from ours. They move through our flesh-and-blood world and wield real power in it" (Gottschall 144). Fairytales and other stories that have been in our world longer than many people can remember have left their own marks on our world that grow larger with every child that they can get to believe. Cinderella specifically, has grown to be larger than life, and the fact that she appeals to the younger generations gives her power over what they believe to be true. In other words, her voice holds a certain level of credibility to where when she speaks, her audience listens regardless of what she is saying, or how she says it, with no questions asked. So for generations to come, Cinderella will have countless numbers of little girls blindly forcing their mothers to buy lavish crowns, ball gowns, blonde wigs, and toy princes in order to become as much like Cinderella as possible because they don't understand that they're being corrupted.

## Works Cited

Gottschall, Jonathan. *The Storytelling Animal.* New York: Houghton Mifflin, 2012.

Zaniya Bass
Heather Hughes
Comp 1
11 Nov 2014

Annalise Keating (Viola Davis) from *How to Get Away with Murder* has a negative impact on female African American adolescents because Annalise Keating causes her audience to think that a woman cannot be successful unless she sacrifices interpersonal relationships. From the outside looking in Annalise seems to have it all. She is one of the most successful defense attorneys there is. She teaches classes at a law school where a select few are chosen to intern for her firm, and she has a husband who is one of the top professors at the school he teaches at. In reality, although she wins almost every case she takes on, she is not afraid to manipulate the system. The students that she chooses from the class she teaches do most of her work for her and she simply takes the best idea. Her and her husband are both cheating on each other and they have no children.

Annalise Keating, although a successful black woman, is constructed almost entirely on racial (black) stereotypes. She has a curvy figure. She wears a wig and fake eyelashes; fake hair is commonly associated with black women. She has an attitude and even though she is smart, she comes off hard and cold hearted. Black women are often times associated with loud mouths and bad attitudes. Often times tv series cannot win for losing. If they do not include "black" stereotypes then the character is not "black" enough. If they do include stereotypes then the character is not cutting edge enough. This can confuse the audience. The audience may be inclined to feel that black stereotypes are unavoidable or they may feel that black stereotypes are poisonous and to run far away from them. Mike Rugnetta explains, "Because from a very young age we're taught to recognize fictional characters and abilities but NOT fictional interpersonal relationships, social dynamics, or portrayals," (2). This quote says that although the audience knows that the show is not real, they may feel that the way that Annalise is portrayed socially is. The audience may feel that these black stereotypes are real obstacles that are contributing to Annalise's failure in her interpersonal relationships.

Zaniya Bass
Hughes
Comp 1
11 Nov 2014

Secretly Broken

From the outside looking in Annalise Keating seems to have it all. She is one of
the most successful defense attorneys in Philadelphia. She teaches classes at a law
school where a select few are chosen to intern for her firm, and she has a husband
who is one of the top professors at the school he teaches at. In reality, although she
wins almost every case she takes on, she is not afraid to manipulate the system. The
students that she chooses from the class she teaches do most of her work for her
and she simply takes the best idea. Annalise and her husband both cheat on each
other and they have no children. As a result, Annalise has a negative impact on
female African American adolescents because these problems cause her audience
to think that a woman cannot be successful unless she sacrifices interpersonal
relationships.

Annalise Keating, although a successful black woman, is constructed almost
entirely on racial stereotypes. She has a curvy figure. She wears a wig and fake
eyelashes. Fake hair is commonly associated with black women. She has an attitude
and even though she is smart, she comes off hard and cold hearted. Black women
are often times associated with loud mouths and bad attitudes. Bad attitudes are
then usually translated to bad relationships because no one wants to interact with
anyone with a nasty attitude. Often times tv series cannot win for losing. If they
do not include "black" stereotypes, then the character is not "black" enough. If they
do include stereotypes, then the character is not cutting edge enough. This can
confuse the audience. The audience may be inclined to feel that black stereotypes
are unavoidable, or they may feel that black stereotypes are poisonous and to run
far away from them. Mike Rugnetta explains, "From a very young age we're taught
to recognize fictional characters and abilities but NOT fictional interpersonal
relationships, social dynamics, or portrayals," (2).In other words, although the
audience knows that the show is not real, they may feel that the way that Annalise
is portrayed socially is very believable. The audience may feel that these black
stereotypes are real obstacles that are contributing to Annalise's failure in her
interpersonal relationships.

The most important of relationships in a woman's life is the relationship she has
with her husband, and, sadly, Keating's marriage is falling apart. Her husband, a

white professor, tends to cheat on his wife with his students. These students are all young, white females. Annalise also engaged in an affair of her own after putting up with the constant cheating of her husband for years. Unlike her husband, Annalise had an affair with a black man. This dynamic is troubling because the Keating's are an interracial couple, yet they cheat with their own color. This is not a coincidence. Writers wanted to emphasize the fact that these two were the wrong two to get married in the first place. It is almost as if the writers were mocking the relationship by implying that they would have been happier if they married within their race. This shows African American female adolescents that interracial marriages, although socially acceptable, do not really end up working and that in reality races should not mix.

Throughout the entire season there is not one person that Annalise trusts enough to consider a friend. Her social life does not exist, and she never does anything that is not work related. She has no one to call when she is unsure or unhappy. So instead of talking out her feelings, she decides to pretend that they do not exist, putting something else on the shelf that is bound to give in at some point. For example, instead of facing the fact that her husband is cheating her and finding a friend that will understand and help her pull through, she decides to get even by having an affair with a police officer. Annalise Keating is alone. She trusts no one and being a defense attorney does not help. Annalise has no real family. She is not close with her remaining living relatives and is not close with the relatives of her husband. Annalise and her husband tried to create a family of their own, but Annalise was unable to bare a child and had multiple miscarriages. Instead of adopting a kid, getting a dog, or looking into other ways of child-like surrogates, she lets it go without telling anyone how much having a child really meant to her. To deal with all of the emotional turmoil that she suppresses, Annalise overworks herself to almost the point of insanity. This shows audiences that Annalise is not strong enough to face her true reality of sadness. Instead, she lets her relationships suffer by pretending that she does not care. This can send the message to the audience that caring is for the weak and Annalise is too strong to care.

The students that intern for Annalise have the upmost of respect for her, yet they do not understand everything she does or why she does it. She is harsh on them and does not have time for messing around. They know that they do most of the work while Annalise seems to be doing nothing. There is no privacy, so she does not have to show the world how lonely she really is. Instead of having an office for her practice, which she can very well afford, she lets the interns and whatever other employees work right out of the entry level of her home. These interns do not have normal 8 to 5 hours and often stay at her house way past 3:00 am. She does not talk to them while the interns are work furiously, unless needed. Yet, she lets them work in her house. I presume that Annalise lets the interns work in her home to create the illusion of closeness for herself. Their presence allows her to pretend she has someone in her corner. The interns respect her but they do not necessarily like her. Annalise tends to fall back on the fact that she is smart and good at what she does. She is an amazing defense attorney and feels that is all she needs in the world. This could send the message that as long as there is respect from people, real relationships and feelings toward them are not necessary. This can cause African American adolescents specifically to strive for fear and respect more than being humble and likeable because humble and likeable are not likely to get the job done.

Annalise holds her education and success in her field near and dear to her heart. As sad as it sounds, without her education she would be nothing. Because Annalise is a black woman, society says that it is not likely that she will finish any form of schooling past a normal bachelor's degree. The fact that Annalise not only graduated law school with honors, but is is one of the best in her field, is the only thing in her life that she is actually proud of. Now, being a successful attorney and graduating with honors is an amazing accomplishment, but there is no sentimental value past a piece of paper and a few won cases. There is nothing that will carry her on or will make her happy after she retires. Being without friends, colleagues, family, or a stable marriage forced Annalise to close herself off to the rest of the world. She refuses to face the true point in the matter.

Annalise Keating has everything that a young African American girl would want from the outside looking in: money, success, and marriage. Mike Rugnetta explains, "The point being: that it's bad because it portrays a world that doesn't exist. And in doing so suggests that the ACTUAL WORLD isn't the way that it ACTUALLY is," (2). Since Annalise Keating is being portrayed as a woman who is successful in monetary value but not socially, she in fact may be telling the world that a woman being successful at both does not exist. Annalise has failed at marriage, family, and friendship. Her students only associate with her because they have to, she cannot let anyone in enough to be her friend, she cannot get her family to communicate with her, and she cannot get her husband to love her. Keating lacks what everyone really cherishes the most: love. Annalise receives no real love from anyone. Success is the only real love that Annalise Keating feels. Therefore, Keating teaches young girls that if one has success and money, everything else that makes a person unhappy can be overlooked. Annalise's success is the same excuse that she uses for failure.

Works Cited

Rugnetta, Mike. "How is Ms. Marvel Changing Media For the Better?" *PBS Idea Channel*. Public Broadcasting Service. 2 April 2014. Web. 18 October 2014.

# Part V:
# Additional Content

# Course Objectives

## University of Central Missouri &
## Department of English & Philosophy

Composition I helps students attain "Competency One" of UCM's General Education Program. For more information about the General Education Program, please visit ucmo.edu/gened. The course also assists students in meeting several Department of English and Philosophy Program Goals. These two sets of goals constitute the course objectives or aims of Composition I. Course objectives normally appear on the course syllabus; we also provide them here.

**General Education Competency One: Writing with clarity and purpose using appropriate conventions of format, structure, and documentation.**

Students will learn that writing is a recursive process that includes both revision and editing. Students will be exposed to formal and informal writing, write multiple drafts of essays, and have at least two individual tutorials with the instructor.

Students will learn to write essays with a clearly stated, well-reasoned controlling idea and will develop this idea and its main points logically and support them with relevant examples, details, data, reasons, etc. They will learn to consider their audience and to organize writing effectively, producing essays that are organized well enough to be easily readable (with a beginning, middle, and end). They will likewise learn to create unified, coherent essays with clearly distinguished and purposely ordered main and subordinate ideas and with purposeful paragraphing and meaningful transitions. They will learn to write essays with few grammatical errors and none that interfere with comprehension and with minimal punctuation, capitalization, and spelling errors. Students will be taught to write essays that adhere to conventional formatting guidelines. In addition, they will learn to think critically about what they read and use evidence and documentation to bolster their own conclusions. In particular, they will employ formal documentation in order to cite correctly other people's ideas to avoid plagiarism. Students will write essays whose in-text citations and list of sources adhere to conventional formatting guidelines.

## English Program Goals

The English Department has adopted a series of goals for its courses. The following goals apply to this course:

- **Expression Goal, Level 1** – Students should be able to write formally and/or informally as situations warrant and distinguish between tentative and polished expression as they develop a personal writing style.

  Students must understand the rhetorical situation and learn to address a variety of scholarly audiences and writing situations. They must distinguish between rough drafts and polished, revised, and edited writing as they cultivate the developing stylistic features of their own writing.

- **Research Goal, Level 1** – Students should be able to understand the purposes of research and documentation.

  Although students will not encounter major research assignments until Composition II, they will be introduced to some of the fundamental principles of documentation and research in Composition I. Students will be asked to use in-text citations as they respond to essays that they have been provided by their instructors. In addition, they will be introduced to MLA style, and asked to cite some of the essays to which they are introduced. In addition, they will be asked to evaluate sources that they are given by their instructor. Finally, they will be introduced to quoting, summarizing, and paraphrasing, and they must understand how to avoid plagiarism and patch-writing in their work.

- **Language Goal, Level 1** – Students should be able to distinguish among levels of English usage—colloquial, informal, formal, literary—and between the nature of spoken and written language; understand and apply traditional grammatical terms and rules to their own and others' writings.

Students must be able to determine the level of formality required for given writing and speaking situations. They also must be able to produce writing that conforms to standard written English conventions. They must have an understanding of grammar and punctuation standards and must be able to edit their own and their peers' writing for mechanical issues.

# Scoring Guide for Composition

## Department of English & Philosophy

**I.**  **Content**

**Exceptionally skillful (excellent)**: Clear, well-reasoned controlling idea, showing insight into the subject and some originality and thoughtfulness; focused, but showing awareness of the scope and complexity of the subject, including possible qualifications and opposing positions; convincing development and support through examples, details, reasons, etc., aptly related to the main points; helpful background, definitions and explanations provided; sources are used effectively and in the service of the writer's argument; impression of thoroughness and completeness in parts and whole.

**Effective (good):** Clear and reasonable controlling idea, good understanding of the subject, with some awareness of its scope and complexity as well as possible qualifications and opposing position; satisfactory and relevant development and support by details, etc., clearly related to main points; necessary background, definitions and explanation provided; sources are used appropriately and in the service of the writer's argument; generally good impression of thoroughness and completeness.

**Competent:** Clear controlling idea and indication of main points, understanding of the subject (though perhaps unimaginative or pedestrian); generally satisfactory development and support by details, etc., related to main points; some attempt to provide necessary background, definitions and explanations; reasonable balance between original arguments and material from sources; attempt at thoroughness.

**Minimally Acceptable (weak):** Evident controlling idea and some relevant supporting points, but may lack focus or clarity; general or superficial understanding of the subject; some attempt at development by details, etc., or background explanation; sources control argument or are almost entirely absent; only partial sense of completeness; argument may be one-sided.

**Unsatisfactory (failing):** Attempt at a controlling idea but vague, overly general, or incomplete; almost no awareness of the scope or complexity of the subject; inadequate or haphazard attempt at development by details, etc., essay may be basically either a summary or a personal argument; repetition or wordiness may replace development; general sense of incompleteness.

**Wholly inadequate (failing):** No sense of the subject, or essay may be off the topic; no discernable controlling idea or haphazard response; little or no attempt at development or explanation.

## II   Organization

**Exceptionally skillful (excellent):** Carefully structured, unified and coherent essay; clear distinctions and relationships among main and subordinate ideas; paragraphing is used strategically, for rhetorical advantage; effective use of transitional devices to link source material to discussion; easy flow from one point to the next.

**Effective (good):** Clearly structured, unified and coherent essay; main and subordinate ideas clearly set forth and related; logical presentation and ordering of points; effective and orderly paragraphing; smooth and informative transitions between source materials and discussion; sense of beginning, middle, and end.

**Competent:** Structure is generally unified and coherent; clear main and subordinate points; reasonable ordering of ideas; appropriate paragraphing; satisfactory transitions; sense of beginning, middle, and end.

**Minimally Acceptable (weak):** Some sense of structure, unity and coherence, or structure may copy that of one of the sources; main and subordinate points may not be clearly indicated; effort at paragraphing may be mechanical or otherwise inappropriate; little clear sequencing of ideas; source material weakly or unclearly linked to the discussion; transitions may be confused or absent.

**Unsatisfactory (failing):** Little sense of structure; unity and coherence marred by omissions and irrelevancies; main and subordinate points, if any, confused or unrelated; little or no attempt at sequencing of points; transitions missing or unclear; may lack an introduction or a conclusion.

**Wholly inadequate (failing):** No structure; disunified and incoherent; no attempt at sequencing or transitions.

III. **Audience, Voice, and Style**

**Exceptionally skillful (excellent):** Argument is clearly directed to and adapted for a specifically visualized reader; effective use of rhetorical strategies to achieve purpose; consistent and appropriate tone and point of view; precise and even vivid use of words to express subtleties of meaning; full command of complex sentence structure; correct and effective use of parallelism, subordination, word order, etc; sophisticated vocabulary.

**Effective (good):** Evident awareness of reader; use of rhetorical strategies to achieve purpose; consistent and appropriate tone and point of view; command of sentence structure; precise and apt word choices to convey meaning; mature range of vocabulary; effective control of sentence structure and variety to convey meaning and emphasis; correct and apt use of parallelism, subordination, word order, etc.

**Competent:** Indications of awareness of reader; some attempt at rhetorical strategies in relation to purpose; generally consistent tone and point of view; consistently correct use of parallelism, subordination, word order, etc., in relation to meaning; appropriate vocabulary;

**Minimally Acceptable (weak):** Some vague awareness of reader; rhetorical strategies, if any, may be inappropriate to reader, subject, or purpose; possible inconsistencies in tone; word choice may lack precision; sentence structure may lack variety; vocabulary may be limited; passages may be paraphrased from sources; essay may rely on authors' language.

**Unsatisfactory (failing):** No awareness of reader; rhetorical strategies, if present, are mechanical or inappropriate; inconsistent, unclear, or inappropriate tone; essay may rely on unattributed quotations; vague or incorrect word choices; limited vocabulary.

**Wholly Inadequate (failing):** No awareness of reader; inappropriately personal voice or nearly complete reliance on sources' language; many inept or wrong word choices; very basic vocabulary.

IV. **Grammar, Spelling, and Punctuation**

**Exceptionally skillful (excellent):** Mastery of conventions of grammar, spelling, punctuation, with almost no errors; sophisticated punctuation.

**Effective (good):** Few and minor mistakes in grammar, spelling, or punctuation; Shows mastery of a range of . punctuation devices.

**Competent:** Some minor mistakes in grammar, spelling, punctuation; grammatically correct relation of all elements of the sentences.

**Minimally Acceptable (weak):** Generally correct basic sentence structure; frequent mistakes in grammar, spelling, and/or punctuation.

**Unsatisfactory (failing):** Errors in basic sentence structure; frequent mistakes in grammar, spelling, and punctuation.

**Wholly inadequate (failing):** Many sentence structure errors that interfere with meaning; many distracting errors in grammar.

# Academic Honesty Policy

## University of Central Missouri

Honesty in all endeavors is essential to the functioning of society. Honesty in the classroom among students and between students and faculty is a matter that should concern everyone in the university community. Indeed, academic honesty is one of the most important qualities influencing the character and image of an educational institution. As higher education is challenged to improve the quality of its programs, there is great value in emphasizing academic standards and integrity.

I.  Honesty

    A.  University Responsibility: It is the university's responsibility to provide an educational process that informs both students and faculty of their rights and responsibilities regarding such important matters as cheating, plagiarism, and professional ethics. Most of what is considered unethical or dishonest behavior can be avoided if faculty and students clearly understand both what constitutes these practices and their consequences. The university community should also be aware of the procedures to be followed should a breach of academic honesty occur.

    B.  Student Responsibilities: Students must be aware that the consequences of violating standards of academic honesty are extremely serious and costly and may result in the loss of academic and career opportunities. Students found to have committed violations against academic honesty face removal from university classes and degree programs, and/ or suspension from the university, while remaining fully responsible for payment of current and any past due tuition and fees.

To that end, the following Procedures for Enforcement of the University's Academic Honesty Policy shall be followed to ensure that constitutionally required due process safeguards are extended to an accused student.

II.    Procedures for Enforcement of the University of Central Missouri's Academic Honesty Policy.

    A.    Defining Offenses Against Academic Honesty

A violation against academic honesty committed by a student is any act, which would deceive, cheat, or defraud so as to promote or enhance one's academic standing. Academic dishonesty also includes knowingly or actively assisting any person in the commission of an offense of academic dishonesty.

Examples of offenses against academic honesty include, but are not limited to, the following:

1.    Plagiarism - Plagiarism is defined as the borrowing of ideas, opinions, examples, key words, phrases, sentences, paragraphs, or even structure from another person's work, including work written or produced by others without proper acknowledgment. "Work" is defined as theses, drafts, completed essays, examinations, quizzes, projects, assignments, presentations, or any other form of communication, be it on the Internet or in any other medium or media. "Proper acknowledgment" is defined as the use of quotation marks or indenting plus documentation for directly quoted work and specific, clearly articulated citation for paraphrased or otherwise borrowed material.

2.    Cheating - Includes, but is not limited to, those activities where a student (either on campus or online):

(a) obtains or attempts to obtain pre-knowledge content of an examination;

(b) copies someone else's work;

(c) works in a group when the student has been told to work individually;

(d) uses unauthorized reference material in an examination;

(e) has someone else take an examination.

(f) has someone else complete course work and/or an examination using a student's secure log in and pass code.

3. Breach of Standards of Professional Ethics - In certain degree programs, students will be instructed on and provided with that particular profession's code of ethics (*e.g. The American Nurses Associations Code for Nurses*). Under some circumstances, if a student is found to have violated that professional code, that violation may be considered a breach of the Academic Honesty Policy.

B. Reporting Violations of the Academic Honesty Policy (revised July 1998) If a faculty member believes that a student has committed a violation of the Academic Honesty Policy with regard to an examination or other assigned work (laboratory assignment, term paper, etc.), the faculty member shall preserve any evidence (e.g. plagiarized article, examination or other material) which substantiates that a violation has occurred. Within one week of the incident, the faculty member will schedule a private conference with the student, advise him/her that the faculty member believes a violation of this Policy occurred, and allow the student to provide his/her side of the story or otherwise offer an explanation. Upon consideration of the information, if any, provided by the student, the faculty member shall make an independent determination within five calendar days whether a violation of the Academic Honesty Policy has occurred. If the faculty member is unable, for whatever reason, to contact the student within a five-class day period, the incident will be reported to the faculty member's department chair for further action.

(1)    In the event the faculty member finds no violation of the Academic Honesty Policy has occurred, the faculty member shall notify the student, in writing, of this finding.

(2)    In the event the faculty member determines a violation of the Academic Honesty Policy has occurred, he/she shall notify the student, within five class days, in writing, of this finding. The written notification shall contain a statement of finding and shall specify the provision of the policy violated and, consistent with the severity of the violation, shall indicate which of the following action(s) he/she shall take:

    a.    Give the student an opportunity to resubmit the assignment or be retested to make up the work or test where the violation occurred;

    b.    Assign a grade of "F" to the assignment or examination affected by the violation;

    c.    Assign a grade of "F" for the course;

    d.    Recommend to the Office of the Vice Provost for Student Experience and Engagement, and the Dean of Graduate and Extended Studies if the student is enrolled for graduate credit, that the student be disenrolled from class;

    e.    Recommend to the Department Chair and the Vice Provost for Student Experience and Engagement, and the Dean of Graduate and Extended Studies if the student is enrolled for graduate credit, that the student be removed from the degree program; or

f.  Recommend to the Office of the Vice Provost for Student Experience and Engagement that the student be suspended from the university.

(3)  In the event the faculty member determines a violation of the Academic Honesty Policy has occurred, the faculty member will provide the Office of the Vice Provost for Student Experience and Engagement a copy of the written notice to the student, accompanied by a summary of all evidence. The faculty member shall keep the evidence and a copy of all summaries and documentation on file in the event the student wishes to appeal the faculty member's decision. The faculty member may interview other students and members of the university community to ascertain the pertinent facts and circumstances and may request written statements from them. However, anonymity of witnesses or witness statements cannot be guaranteed.

(4)  In the event that the student does not appeal the faculty member's decision within ten class days of notification, the faculty member's decision shall become final and the recommended action shall take place.

(5)  A student charged with a violation of this policy shall not be barred from participating in and attending classes, or from taking quizzes, tests and/or final examinations during the ten day period described in paragraph (4) (above) and/or during the appeal process.

C.  Student Appeal Process

In the event a student charged with a violation of this policy disagrees with the faculty member's decision and wishes to appeal, the student is responsible for notifying the appropriate parties where he/she may be reached for purposes of appeal and must follow the following process:

### Level 1 of The Appeal Process

Within five (5) class days of receipt of the faculty member's decision, the student should schedule a meeting with the faculty member's department chair. The chair will review the faculty member's documentation and evidence, review the circumstances with the student, and if possible, consult the faculty member. The chair will determine within five (5) class days of the meeting an appropriate action which may include, but is not limited to, endorsing, modifying, or overturning the faculty member's original decision, or he/she may determine an alternate course of action.

The chair shall communicate his/her decision to the student, faculty member, and the Office of the Vice Provost for Student Experience and Engagement, and prepare a report of the evidence and reasons for making this decision.

### Level 2 of The Appeal Process

In the event the student disagrees with the chair's actions, he/she may request a meeting with the college dean, to be scheduled within five (5) class days of receipt of the chair's decision. The dean will discuss the facts and circumstances of the violation with the student and other involved parties, on a collective or individual basis depending on the circumstances. The dean may also interview witnesses and undertake further investigative activities if he/she believes the circumstances merit further action. The dean shall complete his/her meetings and investigation and issue a finding within fifteen (15) class days of receipt of the student's appeal. In the event the dean is unable to accommodate this time frame, the student and other affected parties will be notified of this fact and the anticipated length of time needed to render a decision. The dean will notify the student, faculty member, chair, and Vice Provost for Student Experience and Engagement of his/her findings, and his/her intended course of action in writing.

### Level 3 of the Appeal Process

If the student disagrees with the dean's decision, the student may request, within five (5) class days of receipt of notification of the dean's decision, a meeting with the Provost. The Provost will consider all the evidence on the record and shall decide, within ten (10) class days to take one of the following actions:

(1)     Uphold one or all of the previous decisions.

(2)     Overturn the decisions outright and make an alternate resolution.

(3)     Refer the matter to a university grievance committee. The Provost
        will appoint a committee of two students and two faculty members
        to review the matter within fifteen class days of the Provost's
        referral. The committee will make its recommendation to the
        Provost within five (5) days of completing its work. In the event of
        a tie vote of the committee, the Provost shall cast the deciding vote.
        The Provost shall immediately, upon receipt of the committee's
        recommendation, notify the student of the grievance committee's
        decision in writing.

The Provost's decision is final and binding on all parties, and once
communicated, shall be placed in full force and effect immediately.
Questions concerning this policy or other issues related to academic
honesty should be addressed to the Office of the Provost or the Office of
Student Engagement and Experience.

# Works Cited

Brandt, Deborah. *Literacy in American Lives*. Cambridge: Cambridge UP, 2001. Print.

Burke, Kenneth. *A Rhetoric of Motives*. New York: Prentice-Hall, 1950. Print.

Clark-Flory, Tracy. "Used Women Are Like Used Cars?" *Salon*. Salon Media Group, Inc., 2016. Web. 17 May 2016.

Elbow, Peter. *Writing with Power: Techniques for Mastering the Writing Process*. New York: Oxford UP, 1998. Print.

Heitkamp, Jan. "Nature Symbolism in the Fiction of John Steinbeck." Diss. N Texas State U, 1971. Print.

Kinneavy, James. *A Theory of Discourse*. New York: Norton, 1980. Print.

National Center on Education and the Economy. Tough Choices or Tough Times.  New Commission on the Skills of the American Workforce, 2007. Print.

National Commission on Writing. *The Neglected "R," The Need for a Writing Revolution*. College Board, 2004. Print.

*P21*. Partnership for 21st Century Learning, n. d. Web. 25 April 2016.

Wade, Lisa. "Sexy and the Gender Binary." *Sociological Images*. University of Minnesota Department of Sociology, 7 October 2011. Web. 25 April 2016.

# Vocabulary Guide

Chapter 1: academic literacy, context, contextualize, decontextualize, decorum, meta-cognitive, rhetorical triangle

Chapter 2: academic literacy, active reader, annotate, commonplace book, multimodal

Chapter 3: clustering, cubing, freewriting, interviewing, listing, looping, outlining, process writing, rough or first draft, word picture, working thesis

Chapter 4: analyze, expressive, informative, persuasive

Chapter 5: climactic, compare, contrast, chronology, patterns of organization, point by point, simple to complex, spatial

Chapter 6: body paragraph, continuity, demonstrative adjectives, development, parallel construction, topic sentence, transitional expressions, unity

Chapter 7: anecdote, conclusion, expository, hook, introduction, summarize, synthesize

Chapter 8: abstract, active voice, concrete, connotation, denotative, diction, passive voice, style, tone

Chapter 9: constructive criticism, edit, global characteristics, local issues, proofreading, revise

Chapter 10: analyze, ethos, evaluate, *Kairos*, logos, pathos, primary audience, purpose, rhetoric, secondary audience, social context

Chapter 11: intertextuality, semiotics, visual rhetoric

Chapter 12: cite, common knowledge, direct quotation, document, in-text citation, paraphrase, patch writing, personal experience, plagiarism, secondary sources, summarize, Works Cited page

A Note on the Readings: contemplation, content, craft

# Index